Ghosts: *Hucknall's Lost Haunted Padley Hall and Other True Hauntings*

– ROY WALTERS –

FASTPRINT PUBLISHING
PETERBOROUGH, ENGLAND

i

www.fast-print.net/store.php

Ghosts: Hucknall's Lost Haunted Padley Hall and Other True Hauntings

Copyright © Roy Walters 2010

ISBN 978-184426-871-9

First published 2010 by
FASTPRINT PUBLISHING
Peterborough, England.

An environmentally friendly book printed and bound in
England by www.printondemand-worldwide.com

Mixed Sources
Product group from well-managed
forests, and other controlled sources
www.fsc.org Cert no. TT-COC-002641
© 1996 Forest Stewardship Council

PEFC Certified
This product is
from sustainably
managed forests
and controlled
sources
www.pefc.org
PEFC/16-33-415

This book is made entirely of chain-of-custody materials

Dedication

I dedicate this book, to Peter and Rita SCIAZKO.
Very close friends of mine.
Peter being of Polish origin, proudly joined the RAF
And served this country well. In the Second World War.

Rita being a spirit Medium, of many years standing, ran her own spiritual centre for many years in the Snenton area, of Nottingham.

Now 89 years young, Rita enjoys semi retirement.

I thank them both from the bottom of my, heart for their friendship and all that Rita as taught me over the years, about spiritualism. I also take this opportunity, to thank my son Lee

For all the help he has given me, to help bring this book together. And I thank everyone who has contributed to this book

Tribute to a Friend, And Friends by Roy Walters

Some three years ago, I lost a good friend, known to all as Ako, who sadly passed away on my birthday, 12th of August, a character, in his own right. I have known Ako ,for over forty years and then some. I feel privileged, to have had a friend like him, he is very much missed.

We have spent many hours, at his home and up the field, just off wood lane, where he kept Rodney his horse, horses were a big part of his life.

We would talk about everything and nothing, I found Ako to be a very deep person, and not many people really understood him, the outside man did not reflect the inside man not by a long way.

I respected who he was and the views, he held, I know he held a lot of respect, for his older brother Roy, who he would always talk about, and always spoke very highly of his sister Karen who I know he loved very much from conversations I have had with him.

We would always get round to talking about life after death, to which he had no belief, he would always say to me, when your dead that's it your dead, there's nothing after, I would always say, no your wrong , but he would not have it, and he said, I would never convince him otherwise .

I remember, one day he said to me laughingly, if there's anything after death , if I go first I will come back and let you know, and believe it, or believe it not , he done just that .

It was about a week or so after his funeral, I had just sat down in my chair at home , to do a bit of a meditation, when as clear as a bell , I heard Ako, say to me , you're doing this are you?.

He went on to say something else, but within seconds, I could not remember what he said to me, I have tried so hard to recall what he said , but I just cannot remember, only the first part , when he said you're doing this are you . It's as if what he said to me has been purposely removed from my mind, for some reason or another, His voice was very sharp and crisp even young sounding, on reflection what surprised me was that there were no surprise or eagerness, in his voice, like shouting excitedly, Roy you were right, or telling me about where he was and what it's all like, It was just like total acceptance, from him just like he would talk to me here, the only difference , was his voice it sounded a lot younger , sharper, even crisper .

About a week after this, I was pottering about at home , and I distinctly heard him shout my name, he just shouted Roy, It sounded like he was just a few feet from me, and yet again a few weeks after this , I heard him shout Roy again, this time it did sound a little distant, like he was a little further away, but still very clear, I think he was just letting me know he's ok, and may be his way of saying, yes Roy you were right, I tell you what did amaze me , that was the short time after the funeral , he was able to come back and make himself known to me, and there were no amazement from him that he had died, but was still here , what can say, but still alive, It was just like it was all natural for him . On reflection, I think I was more amazed than he was , and I was the one who was trying to convince him for years, but it was more like he was showing me that I am the one that needs the convincing , well Ako at the end of the day , you're the one that really convinced me, thanks mate.

I have a lot of respect , for this man, and he joins my list of just a few others who I hold in high regard and have the highest respect for, like Pete Booth, Ray Cook, Pete Richardson, Brian Ellery, Chuck, Pete Clayton, Ralph Radford, Rod Ironmonger, Fred Houldsworth, and Gaynor Clayton.

These are who I call real friends, people who have stood the test of time.

THE HALL

the hall that stood
in its darkened past
the hall where secrets hide
the half way house
for spirit and soul
of those that lived and died
eyes that watch
can not be seen
invisible to us all
but by the soul
can be felt
here at padley hall
black horses stand
in scarlet plumes
the ferryiers of the soul
to and fro
they carry the dead
to fire or darkend hole
dark shadows trapped
from years gone by
held tight at padley hall
voices that whisper
through the night
unresting spirits call

By Roy Walters

Echoes of Padley Hall by Roy Walters

DRAWING OF PADLEY HALL FUNERAL HOME IN THE LATE 1800s NOTE THE DOUBLE FRONT DOORS FOR EASE OF MOVING COFFINS IN AND OUT OF THE FRONT ROOM

DRAWING BY ERNEST WALTERS

FRONT VIEW OF PADLEY HALL IE 32 SYLVESTER ST HUCKNALL AS IT WAS IN THE EARLY 1950S THEN OWNED BY SIDNEY WALTERS WHO OPPERATED A WOOD YARD BUSINESS AND VAIRIOUS OTHER BUSINESES FROM THIS LOCATION

Ask most people in Hucknall about Padley Hall, and very few will have even heard of it. A shame really, as Padley Hall, as a lot of History. For some the Echoes of Padley Hall, still loom in the mindand rise from the ashes like the Phoenix Built I presume in the early 1800s, and being on the south side of Watnall Road Padley Hall was built by the Houldsworth family as a family home and later in the years that lay before it became home to many a family MOSTLY ALL DEAD.As this very old large family home was turned in to a funeral home in the late 1800s by John

Tudbury Padley Hall was not a great big rambling mansion as it sounds But was quiet a large house with rooms larger than most Houses of that Time With a fair bit of land and large out buildings and stables to the rear of the Premises. Where it got its name from I don't know and to date have been unable to find out. what I can tell you in all honesty is Padley Hall was very haunted. I will Endeavour to disclose some of the paranormal phenomena that have taken place in this house that became our home in the late 1950s and was very prominent right up until the middle sixties when Padley Hall was finally raised to the ground. In the year 1890 Padley Hall i.e. 32 Sylvester st Hucknall was then owned by charlotte Plumb and inhabited by Frederick Bodsworth and family. The stables adjoining Padley Hall where owned by Thomas Houldsworth . Padley Hall was to become the home and business premises of John Tudbury. Mr Tudbury started his cab firm business in and around the 1890s from number 6 Lambert Hill, Which still stands today, Lambert hill being at the rear of wood lane stores in Hucknall adjacent to spring street school. As Mr Tudburys business grew he needed larger premises so he purchased Padley Hall. By the end of 1898 Mr Tudbury was Trading from Padley Hall as john Tudbury cab Proprietor, landaus, brakes, broughams, Wagonetts, Shilleers, and mourning coaches. With priority, centering around wedding parties. All in all a very lucrative business for Mr Tudbury and Family for which he must have been very proud. Unfortunately Mr Tudbury had a serious falling out with his oldest son William which resulted in William leaving the family business and working for a competitor which obviously added fuel to the fire, their problems never resolved and father and son never spoke again . John senior died in 1918 leaving four sons, there was William' James' Joseph' and John. Sadly James did not enjoy good health . Joseph his other son died from his wounds at the end of world war one. John junior carried on with the business at Padley Hall until his death in 1951. In the year 1918 john junior married, His wife being Florence may shooter nee Williamson who had a son Thomas from a previous marriage. John and FLORENCE did not have any children of their own but when john's younger sister Freda died in 1924 she left two sons. John and his wife Florence looked after the children and later went on to adopt the youngest of the children who was also named john. In 1958 Florence died and left the estate to her son Thomas from her first marriage . I presume with the death of john Tudbury in 1951 or there abouts Padley Hall ceased to be a funeral home

padley hall

old stables

aerial view of the back of padley hall drawn by ernest walters former resident in the 1950s

stables

work sheds

houses on trueman street

Sid walters bought padley hall in 1956 and ran a wood yard business from these premises

Falling back through my mind I land on the door step of Padley Hall over half a century on, It gives me shivers down my spine even now. We are walking back to the year 1956 when we moved from 25 James Street in Hucknall Which had been my family home for the first few years of life . Dad had now bought Padley Hall which was formerly john Tudburys funeral home in the 1890s but now it was to become our home. Dad had bought Padley Hall for its size and all its out buildings so he could expand his one man wood yard business which he had started in a small shed at the bottom of the garden at 25 James street while working at Linby colliery in between doing chimney sweeping and French polishing and other business ventures . Dad had bought 25 James Street, also the property next door as well which he rented out to a Mrs Sheldon. with dads business expanding, also his family ,I being number seven ,then it was time to move And what a move that was, a move that none of my family will forget. Because here at Padley Hall is where Ghosts poltergeist shadow people and everything else that goes bump in the night entered all our lives and I would go on to say even scar our lives, my younger sister Sharon in particular, Sharon who was born at Padley Hall had the most frightening experiences of all. Sharon who now lives in New Zealand has becomea spirit medium and has more understanding of the paranormal, but at the time was terrified of the goings on in Padley Hall . How many bodies passed through this funeral Home I shudder to think, the young ,the old, Children ,even babies and some I presume in horrific circumstances and this was now our home. A home where you always had the uneasy feeling you was being watched and being watched you where. Turning back the pages of time in my mind, back to when I was about seven or so, I was at the bottom of the stairs just about to go up ,as I looked up the stairs a very black shape of a person, I would say a man, strode across the top of the stairs from my bed room towards the bathroom and my brother Roberts room, there were no features just the dense black shape of a man Like a shadow but much blacker and denser .No I did not go up the stairs I went like a jack rabbit the other way. Dad and Mam were aware of a lot of things that took place there but said little at the time and dads answer to it was just tell them to p--- off they not bother you, so clearly he knew a lot of what was happening . I used to get in bed close my eyes and pretend I was not there under the blankets hiding from footsteps walking across the bedroom floor but nothing there to see. But feeling something or someone sit on the bed feeling their weight push down on the bed but never feeling their weight lift back up off the bed. I sweated my head off many a time under them blankets to scared to come up for air and neither would you if you was there .I got that scared it used to send me bandy legged . You think all sorts of things like if you jump out of Bed you think a pair of black hands will shoot from under the bed and grab your legs all sorts of thoughts go through your head. I reckon I walked about half the time with my eyes Shut so I would not see anything but that did not really work. I know my older brother Robert who is no longer with us experienced on many occasions someone sitting on his bed and trying to pull the covers off him even to the point of being pulled out of bed on to the floor, and the same thing happening again once he had got back in to bed, pulled about by unseen hands you never Knew what was going to happen next or when . The ghostly goings on at Padley Hall seemed to happen anytime day or night and at any time of the year Like the time my older brother Arthur was working in the wood shed chopping sticks, and getting them ready to be bundled up when he saw a disembodied hand waving at him ,he was working on his own in the shed at the time and the only exit out of the shed was to pass the saw bench where he had just seen the hand waving at him but that was the only way out so that is the route he took and I presume a lot faster than any ghost could go, I am not going to say anything about him screaming as that might embarrass him so MUMS the word . My younger sister Sharon also saw a hand waving at her from the bathroom window, a truly terrifying experience for any one let alone a young child. On speaking to a Mavis o Riley a short while ago, she lived on orchard street about 150 yards or so from Padley Hall in the very early 50s just a few short years before dad bought Padley Hall . She tells me that it was rented to two sisters for a few years the sisters being Maydia Digman and her sister Vista, these sisters being spirit mediums. I bet they spent many a hour contacting spirits there, and I bet they drew a lot of earth bound spirits to Padley Hall, they would have been drawn like moths to a light bulb . And who knows what was manifested there, they most probably opened portals for spirit to enter but failed to close these portals properly thereby allowing spirit to come and go as they pleased . And from the goings on in Padley Hall a lot of these spirits would be from the lower regions of the spirit realms. Dark souls who are not at Rest and never will be until they cross over in to the light, I will expand on this a little later. Life there was very hard as a kid, many a winter's night I woke up shivering with the cold, there was no heating in the house, bare wooden floor boards, old coats and old rag pegged rugs I had made myself were thrown on the beds to try and keep warm and if you ever wanted to go to the toilet in the night what a mission that was, the only toilet was outside across the yard in total darkness, no lights out there or in the toilet or should I say old broken down brick building with half the wall missing and most of the roof as well which had tried to stand there since the house was built, no I am afraid it was a bowl under the bed for those sort of activities . Winters were winters then not like they are today I've seen icicles hanging off the roof a foot to two feet long and been there for ages . In 1965 the wood yard was burnt to the ground and Padley Hall came under the slum clearance act condemned unfit to live in. I think it fair to say we did live in squalid conditions. That was how life was then. My older brother Richard says to this day it was a horrible place to live he says he always felt he was being watched someone always there I had this feeling all the time it was like someone wanted to drive you out . Many a time things were thrown about the house by unseen hands I have witnessed this myself. My dad always sat in the hearth as it was one of those big old black fire places with a big built in oven on the side of the fire grate with two smaller ovens at the top, It all got very hot when the fire was lit. Any way there he would sit when he had finished work in the wood sheds, that was his perch so to speak, but he flew off his perch in a hurry one night as, beside him in the hearth was an old brass companion set ,you know ,dust pan brush and tongs on a stand . Suddenly it just flew straight up in to the air as if someone had just had a good kick at it. WOW what a fright they landed on the floor a few feet away then shot up in the air again ,my mam just sat there with her mouth open and the way dad moved out the hearth you would have thought his rearend was on fire . Grabbing the brush and dust pan and shouting go on p--- off get out of it you don't bother me, go on p--- off. I had jumped over on to sofa out the way then the pantry door started banging open and shut like someone was really mad, slamming it shut and pulling it back , it was very frightening . My mam just sat there looking saying nothing and I think I was close to wetting myself . This was hard poltergeist activity . Dad went over to the pantry door shouting d'ya hear go on i've told you to p--- off , get out of it, then it stopped as suddenly as it had started and dad resumed his place in the hearth grinning saying

,see they not hurt you just tell them to p--- off . I don't know if he was scared or what I know I was but telling them to p--- off did seem to work on this occasion. There were other times when dad would come up stairs at night playing hell ,my bed room was directly above his as mam dad and my sister Sharon slept down stairs in the front room , dad thought we was throwing things about and dragging the beds about at night only to find us all asleep, so he must have realised it was poltergeist activity, would go back to bed and my mam would tell us about it next day . A lot of dads friends came from Bulwell or china town as it was called years ago, they would come and work for dad in the wood sheds from time to time, they were always running out of the sheds saying we are not going in there again SID , there are ghosts in there, dad would just laugh and say ha they not ott ya .Many a time they would get all their work done all the sticks bundled up that they had chopped, got them boxed up and stacked only to have all their boxes thrown all over the place in front of them, they would come running out the sheds like little school kids and dad would just laugh. I bet that was the topic of conversation all night when he went out down Bulwell to have a drink with them . There was goings on all over the place in the sheds, in the house ,day or night anytime of the year it was like you were followed about . I was having a bath one day, the bath was at the end of the back bedroom, it was a large room ,I remember you went down some steps to it, I was in the bath, there was not much light just a small window right at one end which did not let much light in, I don't know how old I was may be nine or ten at the time , any way the bathroom door Opened and someone walked down the steps but there was no one there, I could hear them walking about in the room, I sat there in the bath scared to death not daring to move then something came over near the bath, I closed my eyes and thought it could not see me, I never heard it move away, then I heard the bed creaking like it was on the bed or gotten in to the bed then it all went quiet, I must have sat there ages I know the water was very cold and I could not hear anything in the room , then I heard the back door slam shut down stairs, my dad had came in from the wood shed, that seemed to give me a bit of courage so I jumped out the bath grabbed my clothes and shot off into my bed room pulled my pants on and shot down stairs, I told my dad but that was a waste of time ,they not hurt ya, that's all you ever got from him . I don't know what he was thinking of when he bought Padley Hall ,surely there were other places he could have bought unless he got it cheap,I bet nobody else wanted it , it must have come down to money at the end of the day. Good job the cemetery was not included or he would have bought that as well . One night an old friend of the family stayed over, Brian Lee, always a big grin on his face from ear to ear, and he was as rough as an old boot, he stayed in the back bed room ,well bathroom , there was a lot of paranormal activity in this room . On many occasions my brother had all the bed clothes pulled off them in this room ,even to the point of being dragged out of bed and thrown to the floor, and this is what happened to Brian, as soon as he got in bed he felt movement on the bed ,then all the bedding was torn off the bed and thrown to the floor, this happened twice, he wrapped the blankets all around him but then he was dragged out of bed with them, by this time his big grin had gone, he went to sleep in the other room only to have something tugging on the bed clothes most of the night . His big daft grin was back next day ,and he was laughing about what had happened ,but it was a long time before he stayed again. And there was another night when my brother Robert ,Jumped in to bed and flew out as fast as he went in but that was nothing to do with ghosts that night, it was due to the dead mole I put in his bed, that I had found down on the park that day ,well I was only a kid and that's what kids do don't they , you know that was over fifty years ago now and it still makes me laugh when I think about it . This house was a horrible place to live, I can remember hearing my dad telling my mam how he had been pinned down on the bed in the night and he could not move and he could hear an old man breathing , then when all the pressure had gone off him the bedroom door flew open then slammed shut . when you hear your parents talking about things like this it frightens you even more . People talking to dad in the house about what's happened to them in the wood shed and them seeing black shapes of people moving about they don't think about kids sitting there listening ,taking everything in ,they must have thought I was as deaf as a post or something. There were horrible weird animal things in the house as well ,my sister Sharon saw these on many occasions, and my brother Ernest, so I will let them tell you about those things. I suppose these things could have been manifest if someone in the past had been dabbling in the black arts . The back bed room was a cold dark room, I have heard many a time an old man in there clearing phlegm up off their chest and not breathing to well. Over the years I have had a few nightmares about this house, it never seems to leave you ,a couple of weeks ago I was taking some photos of what has been built there now and the very same night the nightmares were back .if it was still standing today I would not set foot in the place not because I am scared now ,I just would not like to feel the atmosphere of the place , and I don't like the memories it still holds for me. As we do not have any photographs of this house my brother Ernest has done sketches of the house which are correct in every detail. Many an hour he has spent working on these drawings and at times has felt rather uneasy as he has felt the presence of spirit around him and at the back of him, I presume watching, and may be even reminiscing , as the drawings of Padley Hall have been resurrected in mind and on paper. Even my brother ken has felt spirit around him ,when I gave him to read what I had written he put it down and would not read any more as he felt too uneasy with it . Six months ago I acquired an old photograph of the late john Tudbury and his son from the late 1800s. I sent this photograph to my sister Sharon in New Zealand ,as soon as she saw this photograph she instantly recognised john Tudbury as she had seen him many a times around the house and out buildings of Padley Hall when she was a child of five years or so ,she was terrified and came over all shaky when she saw this photograph, it had a profound effect on her As Mr Tudbury had died years before she was even born. She was shaken to the core with seeing the photograph and all the buried memories came flooding back for Her. I asked if she would contribute some of her experiences, she very reluctantly agreed but added she did not want to go there in mind body or soul so I left it up to Her. Perhaps Padley Hall is best left in the ashes of the past.

The photograph here shows John Tudbury with his son William taken around 1898 It was taken on Sylvester street just below Padley Hall to the left of Sylvester street you can see Sylvester terrace where the old lamp post stands and to the back of the carriage running along the bottom of Sylvester street you get a glimpse of Orchard street.

Photo provided by Jenny Tudbury

Second photo shows John Tudbury outside of Padley Hall
Photo provided by Susan Hickling of Skegness

Looking back to years gone by the land where Hucknall's police station now stands

Was once where the crematorium and grave yard stood.

And shamefully some grave stones are now used as paving stones.

Just to the rear of the police station stands Munks garage it is believed that an old crypt lies there adjacent to Derbyshire lane

The green dragon public house adjacent to the police station on Watnall road

Stands next to the old cemetery and crematorium Just over the road some eighty odd feet away from the green dragon lies the entrance to Padley Hall where the bungalows now stand

Many have heard, the echo
Of hooves on cobblestone
Dark horses of the night
From Padley Hall, still roam

They ferry too and fro
Over Watnall road
Behind the old Green Dragon
To graves, the graves of old

Deep in the ground, some lie at rest
While others roam the night
On Watnall road some are seen
Shadows of misty white

Some have walked on Curtis street
Others on Truman drive
Some head back to Padley Hall
Where they try to hide

Some revisit the old Green Dragon
In passage and on stair
Toilet area of this pub
Some have felt cold fear

In 1957

A lady from toilet ran
Screaming on the street
She had seen a spirit man

They said it was the beer
That she had drank too much
But then a man took to his heels
Trembling from a ghostly touch

Dark shadows have been seen
Standing just out side
Old customers of the Dragon
That has long since died

Padley Hall By Sharon Walters

I am the only daughter of Sydney Alfred Walters of 32 Sylvester St Hucknall Nottingham England, 32 Sylvester St was once known by the name of Padley Hall, it was an old funeral home owned by John Tudbury. Mr Walters took over the property sometime around September 1956, I was about three months old at the time, and spent the first ten yrs of my life living there. It was not the nicest place for a child to grow up as many unusual events took place in that old house. I lived there with my mother father and seven older brothers, each one of them has their own story to tell, my bedroom was the room downstairs directly next to the big front doors where the coffins were brought in, I understand my bedroom was used as a viewing room where the coffins were stored, I saw many disturbing events in that room when I was very young, around the age of five years old I remember being afraid to go to bed by myself at night and was very afraid of the dark, so my mother would leave the bedroom light on and stay with me till I went to sleep. I remember lying in bed at night and seeing the strangest animals you could ever imagine, one night I was in bed and I saw a strange animal run past my bed and disappear right through the wall on the other side of the room, the animal looked rather like a skinned chicken that was ready to go in the oven, as it ran it's back legs banged together and made a sound like a clicking noise, it was rather scary and I remember hiding under the blankets not daring to move or make a sound, I knew from past experience it was no good screaming because I got so frightened that no sound came out when I tried to scream. Often at night I would lie in bed and hear the front doors open it was very distinct because the door had a huge iron bar across it, so when it was opened the bar had to be removed before the door could open, then I would hear the door close the bar put back in place and several footsteps going up the stairs, then silence, I knew my family were all watching TV and no one had really come in at all, only those not of the earth plane. During the night it was a common occurrence to hear one of my brothers screaming out from upstairs one bedroom in particular was not so friendly the boys would be yelling to each other as they held tightly onto the blankets on their beds, while some unseen force tried to rip the blankets off the bed, they were often grabbed by their feet and an unseen force would try to pull them out of their beds. And often at night I would feel someone sit on the bottom of my bed but there was no one other than myself in the room. Lights would turn on and off, taps would turn themselves on and off life at Padley Hall was not the nicest place for any child to grow up. But to me it was home, and I eventually lost my fear of the unseen spirits.

Continuation by Ernest Walters

My first experience of Padley Hall was with my brother Robert in August of 1956,when we spent the first night of residence together in the house; 32 Sylvester st. Hucknall.

We had been there with my Dad the previous weeks to partly furnish the house and start to equip the business premises that were to become woodsheds, , storage sheds, garages and storage ground; both within the yard and also at the rear for timber, etc-railway sleepers, wooden packing cases, demolition wood.

We were a large family; Mam Dad seven lads and one girl! Mam had had Ten children in total, of which one, a boy named Robert and one, a girl named Pauline, both passed away shortly after birth; Mam then went on to have another son, which she also named Robert.

My first night's residence at Padley Hall, as i can dimly remember, was a cold, nervous affair, as was my older brother Robert's, who sadly passed away a few short years ago.

I cannot recall at that particular time, any untoward events, but that situation , sadly, was not to prevail for very long after the family had moved and settled in the premises! .

I was thirteen years old when we moved in to Padley Hall and spent the next four and, a half years there until I joined the Army 60th Rifles on a nine, year engagement in February 1961.

Both myself and all the family experienced some very strange, unnatural / supernatural and very nasty events, both inside and also outside, in the woodsheds, garages, which were formally stables.

These paranormal events continued whilst I was in service and continued up until the house was vacated by my family in 1966 after a huge fire, which demolished all the out buildings .

One evening my younger brother John , along with another younger brother Arthur experienced a very loud swishing sound going round and round the bedroom very fast , it was like the sound of wallpaper being torn from the walls, but nothing was at all visible.

This continued for a considerable length of time a very frightening experience!

My younger sister Sharon , who moved to New Zealand around 1976 , also had some horrendously frightening experiences in that house as a young child.

I think my first experience of unnatural events began when I was about thirteen and a half to fourteen, with feelings of real cold sensations, even in the living room at night when we had a large log fire and it was really warm.

Dad used to sit in the hearth in front of the fire, falling asleep until his cloths were almost smoking!

I remember doing that one night when I was fifteen and had just had a new raincoat bought me for my Birthday!

I was sat on the hearth with the fireguard up until someone shouted out that I burning! Sure enough! I was! I jumped up and took my new rain coat off and there was a big brown scorch mark and hole half way up the middle!

I very often had the feeling that someone was watching me; nearly always from behind.

This feeling often seemed to be prevalent often in daytime as well as night time and was very unsettling; sometimes very frightening as it was so strong!

I know some of my brothers also had these experiences at times , even though it was not talked about a great deal, but this was in the relatively early days of our occupation of Padley Hall.

When people talk of poltergeist activity these days in our so called enlightened times , they like to try and connect and associate these activities with phrases like' the id, masochism,ect; all derived from the sexual traits and essential drives of our physical and mental makeup and so excused as inhibited teenage sexual frustration or even adult sexual frustration and/ or repression of one of if not the most basic and fundamental and strongest, most necessary drives of all living creatures; the urge to pro-create.

The reason I bring this point to mind is because of the incredible amount of unaccountable, unnatural / supernatural, frighteningly, sheer nasty activities and events that encounted by my family (and others) whilst we were in occupation at Padley Hall.

My own personal experiences, as stated, continued to increase in frequency and intensity over the next two to three years; especially after I had moved from the large bedroom where my brother Robert and several of my younger brothers slept, the bathroom which was situated over the kitchen overlooking the back yard , garages and wood sheds , ect and just contained a bath and one single bed, which I occupied for about two and a half years.

Usually these activities would start shortly after I had been in bed; still with the light on and I would feel cold patches around my neck, Backs of legs would suddenly feel very cold and my back would start a kind of twitching movement.

I would feel weight on my legs and then movement, as if an animal, a dog or something was walking up and down my legs! By this time I was usually frightened and almost unable to move most of my body.

Then the pressure would increase and move up to my chest and upper body, so that I was virtually paralysed and could not speak or shout, even though I tried many times.

Weight and pressure would increase as if a very large man was sitting over my whole body trying to crush me!

May, be this sounds like some form of catatonic trance, but the previous events leading up to these activities do not.

This would go on for ages, I did not really have any idea of the length of time of this activity; (or what I eventually came to term ' visitations'!

I would lie there trying to say a prayer or appeal to some God, or just to try and cry out for help,but either nothing came out of my mouth, or no ever seemed to hear me.

As times went on and the ' visitations' continued, I used to swear and use really strong expletives as foul as I could and sometimes it actually worked! After telling ' it' to clear off, not as polite as that, by a long shot! And then the activity would cease.

Sometimes it did work and I must have fallen asleep out of sheer exhaustion.

I had usually been working for my Dad most evenings in the woodshed, or out delivering sticks, and logs as also were some (and eventually) all of my brothers.

Often we came home from school then worked in the sheds.

These young brothers weren't old enough to experience any sexual frustrations,but did experience very nasty, unnatural events at Padley Hall ; as I have, to a minor extent, outlined in this short narration.

Highbury Vale – by Roy Walters

1.

Highbury Vale, Bulwell, Nottingham, this was the location of my first house which I bought in 1969, being newly married with a baby. The house itself is a three storey building and it lies approximately 200 yards from the church on Highbury Vale.

Money was tight, our baby son Barry had to sleep on a sheepskin rug in a suitcase; we cooked on an open fire in the living room as we had no cooker of our own, and with a lot of hard work in front of me, I put my shoulder to the grindstone and 'got on with it. I was employed as a Metal Polisher at the time.

One of the many 'first jobs' to be done in a new house is decorating, and this we started to do, one room at a time - as and when finances permitted.

Back to the decorating, and one night - after work, doing some papering in the living room and standing on top of the step ladder to do so, I heard a voice say "Hello, that looks nice", I turned round the best way I could and saw an elderly couple standing there.

"Yes, just doing a bit of wallpapering, you know, a bit at a time". The man was looking around him, "You've just moved in then?" to which I answered "Yes, not too long ago."

My wife, Pat, was in the kitchen at the time, and so I thought she'd let them in, for I didn't have a clue who they were. The man said "We were just walking past and thought we'd come and see who was here." My mind was not totally in gear, I'd have probably said something to them about them being here, but it just did not come to mind; then they said a, cheery "goodnight" and left.

No sooner had they gone that my brain started ticking, I said to Pat "Who were they? She said I don't know well you must have let them in". "I didn't let them in, I just turned round and they were standing there;

, tick, tick, my brain was really kicking in now! I was papering in the back living room, Pat was in the kitchen, so the front of the house (which overlooked the main road and the library, was in total darkness, which meant that the elderly couple (who must have been into their seventies) would have to have walked down a long dark entry, come through next doors back gate and into our yard, all in total darkness and without knowing anyone was at home.

We never saw them again, they 'disappeared' as quickly as they had 'appeared', neither of us had let them in, they were just there, and to this day I believe this was a visit from some Spirit people, maybe people who lived at that address at some time, obviously I can't say for sure, but I can think of no other explanation for the mysterious events I've recounted above.

2.

Not knowing what time it was, I was awoken from my sleep one night by the events of a dream. I had dreamt that I'd seen a doctor pulling the sheets over someone who had just died; little wonder it woke me up!

Now for some reason, and believe it or not, I 'just knew' it was my boss's next door neighbour who'd died, I didn't see any face of the person being covered over, I just 'knew' who it was, and just for the record, my boss lived in Sandiacre, some 11 to 12 miles from Bulwell, I didn't even know where Sandi acre was at that time, and I certainly didn't know my boss's neighbour!

Fortunately, morning didn't take long to come round after such a fitful nights sleep, in fact it was soon time to get myself off to work, but the 'death' I'd dreamt of was still playing on my mind.

I got to work about 7:30am, and with being a key holder, I let myself in as I would often make an early start, and most times finish late. It was a small company, only 3 or 4 employees, and our boss had a very easy going nature – he just wanted the work doing.

The boss arrived about 9:00am, dressed unusually enough in a nice suit rather than his work clothes. He came up to me and said "Roy, I'll not be able to stay today, something's come up during the night and I need to sort a few things out, so will you lock up tonight for me please." I said I would, and as I looked at him I said "I know why you won't be here today... your neighbour died during the night didn't he ? With an incredulous look on his face he looked at me and spluttered "How the hell did you know that Roy", I replied "You wouldn't believe me even if I told you. I then said he died in hospital, didn't he? he replied yes he did

3.

Times change, and soon enough I went to work at Linby colliery, having to catch the 5:30am bus from Bulwell to Linby.

One dark and dismal morning I was downstairs in the back living room making the most of an early morning cup of tea whilst getting ready for work. The house at that time in the morning was really quiet, and as I sat for a minute or two I thought I heard the sound of breathing. Almost immediately I saw a bright green ball of light 'fly' up the wall, I couldn't quite believe what I'd seen, a glowing ball of light – green light, and as I saw it, the breathing noise became stronger, it sounded just like an old man struggling to breathe.

Sitting still, for I couldn't have moved if I'd have tried, I held my breath to see if it was my own breathing I could hear, but I could still hear the breathing, to me it seemed to be emanating from somewhere around the fireplace. I gathered my thoughts and things for work, and slowly went for my bus to work, still feeling shaken by what I'd seen and heard.

The following morning, and for near on two weeks, nothing happened, until one morning when I got downstairs and switched the living room light on, for it went straight off again. I flicked the switch again, and this time it stayed on, but now I could hear 'that' breathing again. I must admit that it scared me a little, so I turned as if to leave the room, and as I did so I felt what I can only explain as someone grabbing my arm, maybe not roughly, but grabbing it all the same. Not a nice feeling.

A few days later I was chatting with my next door neighbour, telling him what had been happening in the house, he said "I bet it was Arthur". "Who's Arthur" I asked, "An old chap who lived here, he had a lot of trouble with his breathing, he'd gasp for breath at times, anyhow, he died in your living room, he'd lain in the fire place for about three days before anyone found him".

All told, I lived in that house for about three years, and had no further problems, but I tell you, it did make me think back to when we'd first moved in and we were visited by the elderly couple who came in from nowhere and left the same way.

4.

My wife was starting to feel really uneasy in the house, and to be honest so was I, the house felt cold, I could sense something on the stairs and in the small bedroom, this 'sense' wasn't there all the time, but it was there often enough to put us on edge.

There was one occasion when we asked our neighbours if we might borrow their dog to see if he would go upstairs, it was a little Jack Russell, but this was to no avail, for it was having none of it, for the moment we tried to get it upstairs, it's fur went up and it just about yapped it's little heart out, there was no way would this dog move, so our neighbour took it home to calm it down.

The time had obviously come to do something, so we contacted the church to see what the vicar at that time made of whatever was troubling us.

The vicar duly came round, but felt that he needed to speak with his superiors before returning and saying some prayers. When he did come back, he'd brought with him a silver bowl, some Holy water, a Bible, and a Cross. He said some prayers, blessed the house, sprinkled some holy water, after which he took his leave. However, his actions didn't seem to do much to alleviate what was happening in the house, so I went back to the church to tell them this.

This time a different vicar came out, a big man, not a man to be messed with! He and I sat down, and together we discussed what we'd been experiencing in the house, the breathing, the orbs of light, the 'touching', the sense of foreboding, I lay it all before him and the church to see what he could do for us.

His actions were pretty much the same as the other vicar, only this man went right through the house saying prayers, and sprinkling Holy water about. The result was a few months of inactivity which we were very grateful for, but then it started up all over again.

When things started to 'kick off' again it was one night just after we'd gone to bed, for I just knew that there was something bad outside the bedroom door, and to be honest I was scared, so scared that I started to pray.

As I prayed a warm glow started to draw itself up the bed, from my feet upwards, and as it drew up my body, the room seemed to get lighter, and within what must have been seconds, all the fear I'd been feeling left me for I 'knew' that whatever was outside the bedroom door couldn't get in to us, that we were safe. I lay back feeling relaxed and safe and had the best night's sleep I'd had in ages.

Twenty years passed by, and I had a reading by a local medium (Ann Monks) in which she told me literally everything that had happened that night, she was even able to describe the position of our bed.

She told me that a family member (in Spirit) on my mother's side of the family had come to protect me (us) that night. She was even able to tell me about the breathing we'd been troubled by, that it was a man 'Arthur' who had been trying to contact me as he knew I was sensitive to Spirit presence, that he was sorry for scaring me, that he just wanted to contact me by making me aware of his presence. At least I know he's at peace now.

Events in Whitcombe Gardens – by Roy Walters

1.

Circa 1984/85 I moved into a council house on Whitcombe Gardens in the Top Valley area of Nottingham, It wasn't long however before I was made aware of the presence of Spirit in the house, sensing them mostly either in the bedroom or at the side of the bed, and there were occasions when I'd feel a hand being placed on my forehead as I laid down to go to sleep. It wasn't frightening to experience this phenomena, I felt I was being soothed and that I was to lie back and go to sleep. I've no idea who or what it was that did this, but it certainly wasn't frightening.

Then, one night as I lay in bed, and just as my partner had reached the top of the stairs, there was a sound, it sounded like the rushing of the wind, it 'shot' from the bedroom door, rushed through the room, and hit the curtains - which then started to 'crackle' as if they'd been hit by a bolt of electricity. The curtains were actually shaking, it was almost as if something was behind them – like a trapped bird trying to free itself from a net, but with a loud crackling of electricity.

It's fair to say that I wondered what was happening, and so I leapt out of bed, pulled the curtains apart and... nothing, no reason whatsoever for what I'd just experienced, but the room went suddenly quiet as quickly as it had started, the best way I'm able to describe is to say it was a bolt or discharge of some sort of energy.

Some time after the above event I started to have a lot of nightmares, a recurring nightmare about a 'ghost' who was trying to 'get inside' me – or at least that is my interpretation of it. Then one night as I got into bed I witnessed a ball of bright Red light fly across the bedroom to the side of my bed, I was then able to sense something at the side of me. I couldn't see anything but I could sure feel it's presence, and to be honest it scared me a little as I felt I knew it's intention, it was the nightmare coming true!

More out of temper and nervousness I swore at it and told whatever it was that it couldn't hurt me, (me and my big mouth!), it was at this point that I experienced a sort of rippling sensation in my feet which slowly and deliberately began to rise up my body – from the inside! It continued to rise, right up into my head, at which point it seemed to exit at the crown of my head. The entire event could have only taken maybe 5 or 6 seconds, but it sure felt longer, it was unpleasant, it felt really quite horrible, it was definitely not something I'd want to experience again.

2.

Another instance of Spirit presence in the house occurred one night as I lay in bed, just staring into 'space' when something, some 'big and heavy' energy, tried to "… crush down on me…" Such was the intensity of it, It's difficult to write down how a sound actually sounds, but try whispering the words Har and Shar together – Harshar – and that would be pretty close to the noise I heard as this energy came around me.

Then the thought of my brother-in-law popped into my mind, he'd been tragically killed in a mining accident some years earlier, he was a big man, over six feet tall and nineteen to twenty stone in weight. He'd been crushed in the accident, and this was the sensation I was starting to experience.

It actually felt rather hostile, really unpleasant; it was almost as though he – or whatever it was – was trying to crush me. I couldn't understand why he would want to hurt me as we'd always gotten on well together, in fact we spent a lot of time together and were good friends, so I just didn't understand why he'd be doing this to me. I know now that this could have been his way of letting me know he was around, but at the time it scared me rigid.

I actually started reciting the Lords Prayer, and I have to say that as I prayed I began to feel the weight lift slowly off me until it had left me completely, at which point I leapt out of bed, and went downstairs to make a drink of tea as I felt really shaken by the whole experience.

It's very scary when these things happen to you 'out of the blue', it's also easy to be brave about it after the event, but believe me, at the time it's happening to you, the last thing you feel is brave.

3.

Yet another instance of Spirit activity in the house occurred one day when my son Lee (who was just three years old at the time) and I were alone in the house. It was in the afternoon; he'd fallen asleep, so I lifted him and placed him in his bed. A little while later I went in to check on him and as I walked towards his bed something shot past close by the side of my head, and hit the wall at the back of me with such force that it made a dent in the wall itself.

I looked down to see what the object was, it was one of those small wooden building blocks that children have, yet where it had come from or who could have thrown it – especially with such force – I'd no idea.

Thinking to myself "Don't show any fear" I smiled, picked up the block, and took it into my bedroom to mull things over as to what could have caused this to happen. A few minutes later I went back into Lee's room, woke him up, and took him downstairs, for you see, I'd figured that given the accuracy and speed of the object, it could easily have put a dent in me if whoever had thrown it had wanted to hurt me.

Thankfully, that was the only 'poltergeist' activity I experienced in that property.

4.

And finally, while not exactly Spirit phenomenon, I was one night woken up by a dream – although I wouldn't want to call it a 'dream'. In it, I could see myself looking at the scene of an accident, I could see the car, but there appeared to be no-one there, the air/the atmosphere, was so peaceful, my instinct told me someone had been killed, but there was no sign of who it was.

When I woke up, I looked at my alarm clock, it was just after midnight, and it was really playing on my mind. I told my partner at that time about it, she said "It's just a bad dream" but I somehow knew it was more than that, for I knew someone had died in it.

The 'dream' was on my mind all that following day, it just wouldn't go away - and it was still there when my partner brought the children home from school that tea-time.

She was upset, for while talking with other mum's outside school, she'd learnt that a good friend of ours - who only lived about 200 yards from us - had been killed in a road traffic accident during the night. The time of the accident was about 12:30am, hers was the only car involved, and somehow – though I know not how - she'd hit a tree and been killed instantly. She was only 28!

This then was my dream, and I must have dreamt it either just before or at the same time as it had happened.

Wrong Frame Of Mind

After leaving school in july 1958 at the age of fifteen, my first employment was in a hosiery factory on Derbyshire lane, Hucknall Notts. As an apprentice hand frame knitter. The work seemed not to be physically over taxing and the wage fairly good for an apprentice, but after a couple of months the work seemed to become monotonous and i left to start work as a trainee coal miner!

I really think that one of the factors which subconsciously really decided me to leave was an incident which occurred within a few weeks of my employment!

it was a Friday evening and I was left to finish off some work the only other person working in the shop was a youngish man named Bill from Bullwell, who constantly smoked pigtail twist in a curved pipe. He was working at the other end of the shop to me but on the same side and as the knitting frames were close together and facing in the same direction I could not see him; only hear the clacking of his machine

the frame immediately to my front was worked by Mr Wiles, (not his real name!) a balding, middle aged slim man who was usually quiet yet always a pleasant conversationalist, He had said goodnight to me perhaps an hour earleier, as he always finished at 5.30p.m on a Friday, immaterial of wether his work was actually completed or not.

about an hour and twenty minutes after Mr Wiles had left, I was still working away on one of the mohair shawls I was knitting, when suddenly I felt a sort of tingling sensation over the upper part of my body and head! I gave a little shiver and carried on working, but less than a minute later I felt the air about me was really cold and I shivered again, at the same time as giving a half glance to my right and the centre aisle between the frames. There seemed to be a black shadow or form standing in between my frame and Mr Wiles and looking into his frame! I only got the one glance at it for a few seconds, as it had vanished by the time I had blinked and looked again!

The figure seemed to be clothed in a long black gown belted at the waist with a large black hood covering the head. I leaned out of the frame and looked all around but there was nothing to see and I could only hear the clanking of the other machine at the far end of the room. I tried to forget the incident, thinking it was probably some kind of hallucination but after about another twenty minutes I had to stop working and go home.

On my return to work the following Monday morning, to a very sad and glum atmosphere, I was almost immediately informed that the man who worked in the next frame to me had committed suicide on the Friday evening after leaving work!

My mind flashed back to the incident on Friday evening and I felt shocked and sick and asked to be excused work for that day as I was under the weather. The next day I returned to work for another fortnight behind the empty frame.

By the end of this time I had convinced myself that the work was to monotonous for me to carry on and I handed in my notice!

the last week I worked on different machines in other shops I never mentioned the Friday evening incident to any one or discussed it with anyone but I can still see that black form/figure now fifty two years later ,even as I write and it is as plain as the paper in front of me, indeed as plain as the moment I saw it between the frames that Friday evening.

True account of ghostly apparition
In July 1958
At R.L Jones Derbyshire lane Hucknall
Hosiery factory
By Ernest Walters

At the age of fifteen and in the employment of R.L Jones
Ernest was living at
PADLEY HALL

Seeing the Soul by Roy Walters

I believe I have looked deep inside two people and have seen or felt their soul. I think to say felt, would be more appropriate and what I found rather strange was the similarity of the events in both cases, i.e. Each time I was crouched down in front of the person and they them self's were in a sitting position and both people being female and on both occasions at the time it was taking place, I consciously Knew it was happening, but did not have the full realisation of it , It's very difficult to try and explain , because when something like this happens in reality, it would knock you for six. It would be equivalent to turning you inside, out literally. But it don't sort of register in your mind till after and you're walking away from them; then the hammer strikes! It hits you just what has taken place. It was like duplicating the experience with the second one. The reason for it happening in the first place I have no idea. First time it happened I was in Sutton in Ashfield attending an auction, where I had been going for many years and I knew the family well that was running the auction. I was crouching down in front of Kate the auctioneer's wife just having a quick word with her. While I was crouched in front of her talking ,all of a sudden I felt what I can only describe as a strangeness about me and it was like looking deep in to her and seeing her soul her real self ,her spiritual self . I'm not going to say I saw her soul. what I am going to say, quiet categorically, is ,{ I felt her soul } It was like a very deep knowing what I felt in those few short seconds; what was reflected back at me was like she was a thousand times better person than what she actually portrays in her everyday life. In every way shape and form, everything about this person was intensified a thousand fold and that is no exaggeration! To feel and experience this would blow your mind, but as I said, you know it, you feel it, [but] the realization of what just took place at the time is not there full- blown, not until I stood up and walked away. Then I understood what had happened. The second time this happened I was in the Nabb Inn public house in Hucknall .A friend of mine who I had not known very long was in there ,I went over to her to say hello, she was sitting down at the time. I crouched down in front of her, and once again while talking to her I experienced this strangeness about me then it was like seeing very deep in to her, just like I had done with the other person a couple of years before. I believe seeing her soul, her true spiritual self, but seeing not with my eyes but with feelings. Seeing with spirit eyes, seeing with the souls eyes; whatever, and once again everything about this person was intensified a thousand fold. It all just flooded in to my mind again. I had looked in to her soul! I may also add that this person I have just written about is now my partner and mother to my children and has been for many years now.

I would not like to look in to a person and see the reversal or feel the reversal of what I saw. Just imagine looking in to someone like Hitler and seeing and feeling all the horrible things about them intensified a thousand times, it would absolutely terrify you!

Hanged Man by Roy Walters

I sat in a spiritual development circle one evening in Mansfield with a very well known professional medium. I think there were about twelve people in this circle who were sitting for development. I went along with my friend who is also a professional medium. We were made very welcome in the circle. And the first evening we did a bit of work using psychometriy. I was given a gold ring to hold belonging to a lady in the group. I held the ring in my hand and almost immediately I saw an old gentleman and a lady in an old house. I described in detail this old couple who she recognised to be her grandparents and she said the ring I was holding used to belong to them. I also described the inside of their house to which she said I was correct, then I saw a jack Russell dog which she said belong to her grandparents. I then went on to tell this lady that her grand farther used to work in the mines but then changed his job and went to work on the railway; she said yes you are right .Next I was given something else by another lady. I quickly described her mother to her and also where she worked, all correct. I also told her that her mother was youngish when she passed, to which I was also correct and it went on and on. I described her son to her and told her about his fourth coming wedding which was being planned at the time which was all correct- all in all, a very successful evening the medium running the circle said I want you to take sealed envelopes home with you and open them when you get home and see what you pick up from what I have placed in the envelopes so I said ok, never thought no more about it . I took the envelopes home and a couple of days later I sat on my bed and opened the first envelope. In it were two glass beads, I held them in my hand closed my eyes and within seconds I saw a plain glass vase in my,mind I couldn't see anything else, so I opened the second envelope took out some small stones held them in my hand and closed my eyes .I saw a very large man with short dark hair wearing a grey leather jacket, walk off a field and look straight at me and started to grin. It was a bit disturbing, as I said, he was a big man must have been six feet two or three, heavy build. Anyway I went back to the group the following Monday and gave her the envelopes back. She said did you pick anything up from them. I said yes, from the first one I saw a plain glass vase. She said that was what my husband gave me for Valentine's Day; I keep those glass beads in it. I said from the second one I saw this big set man described him to her and told her what he done and described his clothes that he had on, but she did not look very pleased. She then said, who you have just described to me is my husband. She then took a photo out of her bag and showed this to me and there he was, the man I saw walk off a field and grin at me, but on the photograph he had longer hair, but none the less it was him. She then told me he was dead, he had committed suicide years ago. She did not say much more, but before I left that evening she said when you come next week I would like you to sit in a cabinet on your own, like they used to do years ago at the old spiritualist meetings. she was doing things the old way, like when we sat in circle it was almost dark with just a small red lamp on, all very spooky . She said, sit in the cabinet and all of us in the group will direct our thoughts and energy at you , I said NO, I don't want to do it ,she said well have a think about it and decide next week .I thought to myself what is she on with . Anyway my friend advised me not to do it. The following week quickly came round and I was asked, again but I was adamant- I was going in no cabinet!. So she said ok, sit out here and we will all send our energies to you from here .still not knowing what she was really up to. Well we formed a circle, the lights went out and she put the red lamp on. I had a quick look round this large circle they all looked very spooky in the red light. I thought to myself, what the hell have I let myself in for, in at the deep end Roy, it all went quiet, not a sound. I took a deep breath said the lord's prayer to myself then put white light all around me and asked for protection from the higher realms of the spirit world, but just did not feel right. I closed my eyes and just let events take their place, I could hear one or two of them breathing, but this seemed to quickly fall away and I started to feel very distant from the group-.like I was being pushed away from them. Then I felt someone really big at the back of me. I started to feel like I was getting bigger and bigger. At one point I felt that big, I thought I was standing up I felt enormous in size. Then I felt myself being bent over to my right hand side I was aware of it but felt along way a way; it was like a very distant feeling. Then I was startled by a woman screaming and running across the floor shouting and crying. I opened my eyes and was very confused as to what was happening around me at this point. I was bent right over, more or less lying across the woman next to me. The lights came on, everyone was looking rather shocked. The medium was right down the other end of the room crying and being sick .to say the least every one was shaken up . When the medium came back and composed herself a bit, she said. I was trying to see if my husband would try and use you to come back, and he did! She said he hung himself and the position I'd been placed in was how she had found him. She also went on to say she couldn't get rid of him, he keeps coming back to try and get her to commit suicide. If this is true or not I don't know, but she said she has had this trouble with him for years and at one stage had given up her work as a medium to stop him coming through, but it had not worked. She went on to say, obviously, he is now going to use you to come back. So I will have to ask you and your friend to leave and not return again. So that is what we had to do. But in all fairness she should have told me what her intensions were right from the start because I felt like I had been used. Well I had been used more by her than her husband. This was round about 2001 I have since seen this medium twice and on both occasions she has ignored me strange woman !

Beauvale Road by Roy Walters

The year 2,000 was fast approaching when I moved in to a property on Beau vale road in Hucknall. And it proved to be the most haunted house I have ever had the misfortune to have ever lived in. It was Padley hall reincarnated; in fact it made Padley hall look like a little pussy cat. Dark forces were at work within the first few hours of moving in to this house. Day one of moving in, I was in the bathroom cleaning my teeth, the bathroom being directly at the top of the stairs. As I stood there brushing my teeth something jumped right in front of my face, just like an inch away. I Automatically jumped back and spun round in fright, only to see a black shape swirl round the bottom of the stairs in just a matter of a second or so from it being right up in my face; it moved so fast it was unbelievable . I cannot say in all honesty that it was a black shape of a man or anything, it was just a black thing and it moved so fast. I did not say anything to my partner Barbara, or the kids. I supposed, well hoped nothing else would happen again or none of them would encounter what I just had. HOW WRONG I WAS! This house turned out to be the mirrored image of Padley Hall. Not at first, but over time dark forces rose, grew in strength and caused havoc among my family. I don't know any history of this house. I spoke to a neighbour who had lived close by for over forty years. She said no one had died in the house while she lived close by or at any other time to her knowledge, but spirit, ghost or whatever you wish to call them was in this house; very much so! At first it was not too bad; the odd loud bang here and there and in the middle of the night sometimes, it would be right at the side of you. It sounded like someone slamming something down very hard and in temper then nothing, all would be quiet .Her indoors, Barbara, is very sensitive to spirit and was on numerous occasions seeing people about the house; people being spirit people. Small incidents were happening all the time, doors opening and closing, footsteps on the stairs. Sounds, as if someone was walking about just above you when there is only you in the house. These small incidents slowly built to stronger incidents. As time went on I was becoming more involved in the paranormal; reading books, attending spiritualist churches; also sitting in spiritual development circles in the churches, also privately. With developing, I was becoming a lot more aware of spirit and certainly knew when spirit was around me. I mixed and worked with a lot of mediums over a long period of time. So a lot of things that happened at Beauvale Road I tended to take in my stride. That was until dark forces, negative energy, whatever label you care to put on it results to violence and believe me they CAN and do! A lot of people wrongly believe spirit cannot harm you they are wrong as Barbara my partner found out first hand. She was violently attacked in this house by unseen forces, which resulted in her head being pushed down in to the bath .and on another occasion was hit so hard in the eye blood was drawn from a half inch cut and swelling and bruising, a truly terrifying experience to which I will come to a little later . As I said, many things happened in this house; doors just opening and closing, the handle on a glass door would go up and down; you could see straight through the door but no one was there.Once I was in the kitchen making a cup of tea and I sensed a child walk round the back of me, then I felt a tug on the back of my shirt; I turned round only to reveal nothing, no one was; there it was like they were playing games with you . Pictures have just flew off the wall for no apparent reason and I mean flew off the wall, not fallen off! One day I was putting washing on radiator to dry in the back room. Out the corner of my eye I saw a little girl, maybe seven to eight years old bob down at the back of an arm chair. It did not frighten me but really startled me, to see it; I pulled the chair right away from the wall to reveal nothing! When I sort of settled a bit, as I said it did startle me; I thought, did I see a little girl? The chair was pushed right up to the wall, so how could I see a little girl bob down at the back of it? The answer to that is, I don't know, but I did see it, it did happen. Strong scents would just blow in your face from nowhere and would be gone just as fast as they came. Another time I was going up the stairs, I was half way up, our Lee's bedroom door was half open. As I looked up I saw a man in navy blue overalls leaning over doing something in his room. I shouted down to Lee and Scott just to make sure that they were down stairs; they both shouted, "What"? From down stairs, so I walked straight in to their bedroom but there was no one there! Another time I was putting washing on the radiators at the bottom of the stairs. My son Lee had just come out of the bathroom and was on top of the stairs going to his bedroom. As I looked up at him, a dark shape of a man just shot right past him! Lee never saw it or felt it. It went straight in to the bathroom but sort of swirled round the bathroom door very fast it seemed an impossible move to make it sort of bended and swirled at the same time right round the back of the door. When it came past Lee it was only inches from him so why did he not see it or even feel it, or was it just showing its self to me? Yet once again .I know it was the same thing I saw when I first moved in to the house, but this time it did have a shape to it, perhaps that's because it's energy was becoming stronger . There was a time when Lee knew something was there as he was talking to my brother in the front room, he was tapped on the shoulder three times. Man! You should have seen him move! If he had been going in a straight line, he would have done a mile in less than three minutes! Boy, he was scared to death! He plonked himself down at the side of my brother ken, who promptly told him," get over there, I don't want it!" I think they were both ready to use the toilet, but then again who would not be. My brother as felt some one around him on many occasions in this house. One Sunday afternoon my sons Lee and Scott went out to visit someone; a little while later my brother John came to visit me we both sat in the back room talking. I went in to my front room to put some washing on the radiators; the curtains where fully open, they would have to be to get the washing on to radiators. My brother never went into this room on this visit. About one thirty I gave my brother a lift over to his mother-in-laws. I had only been out my house I would say less than ten minutes. I locked up when I went out. My sons were about five miles away. When I returned, the curtains in the front room were fully drawn no one else had a key to my house; only myself and my two sons who did not return home till after six o clock that evening . It was just another incident to which I quickly pushed to the back of my mind. lots of things were happening all the time, like this; you would be in the bedroom, all of a sudden there would be a loud bang near you or just away from you like someone had just slammed something down in temper, but there was nothing or no one there. This sort of thing happened on many occasions. One Christmas eve Barbara and my children had just returned from mid night mass Barbara was in the bathroom directly at the top of the stairs I was in my bedroom; my bedroom being right at the side to the top of the stairs and my bedroom door was fully open. Barbara is adamant she heard a man walking up the stairs from just about three to four steps from the top saying quiet clearly," Jezebel bong" . I heard nothing at all. As she heard this man on the stairs, a picture of him formed in her mind. He was in his early forties, of thin build, white open neck shirt, black curly hair. She refers to him as the medallion man, as this was the impression she got of him sort of happy go lucky, like jack the lad character. What Jezebel bong means I don't know? This was repeated twice. It is very clear in her mind, what she heard on the stairs and has never wavered from this over the years .One evening Barbara was going up the stairs to run a bath, but three quarters way up the stairs she saw the figure of a man, sixty to seventy years old sitting on the stairs. Thoughts were being placed in her mind by this man not to go any further. Not to go in the bathroom as she would be in danger! She came back down and told me what had just happened, so I said," Well, take notice then." She was given this message for a reason, but with Barbara being Barbara, she listens to no one. She was determined to go and have a bath, but kept on getting impressed on her not to go beyond the point on the stairs where he was, as it would be too dangerous for her. I told her time and time again to forget the bath and to take notice of the warning she was clearly being given, but she was having none of it and started to get annoyed and insisting she was going to have a bath, a bit like throwing your toys out the pram, but there we are . So I told her not to lock the bathroom door and I would be a matter of only a few feet away in my bedroom Well she went in to the bathroom and washed her hair then put a small amount of water in to the bath; nowhere as much as she would normally put in. She had tied a towel around her head because of her hair being wet but at this stage she had locked the bathroom door for her privacy. This I did not know. As she leaned over the bath to mix the water with her hand, she felt a hand on the back of her head that pushed her head down in to the water, which caused her to hit her head slightly on the inside of the bath, but her head was cushioned by the towel . She had the impression of a young woman about sixteen to eighteen years of age standing to the back of her, next to the sink. Her head was still being pushed down in to the water but she knew this girl was not very strong as she was of frail build so with that Barbara got one hand on the side of the bath and pushed up hard, As she pushed up the pressure of the hand on her head ,and the girl had gone . Barbara screamed. All this took place in a matter of seconds. I got to the bathroom door tried to open it, but it was locked so I just kicked it open. Barbara was in a right state of shock to say the least, and I was fuming with her for locking the door and taking little notice of the warning she had been given- good job she did not fill the bath up with hot water as she normally would have . Never- the –less, she should have still not gone in the bathroom at all that night; she had been warned. It had also given Barbara a right headache but she did not hit her head hard enough to warrant her head hurting in this way as her head was wrapped in a towel from her washing her hair first .This incident was very disturbing to us all can't begin to understand how it was for Barbara, she was terrified. At this point I decided to go and see a friend of mine, a very well known and respected spirit medium. Talking to Barbara he asked her if she knew anyone who had died by hitting their head and drowning to which she said no. We had only left his house a short while and driving home when it came straight to Barbara's mind about a friend of hers and the family; a young girl of seventeen who was involved in a tragic road accident whereby she was knocked unconscious and died by drowning she was a passenger in a car that went out of control and ended up side- down in a ditch at the east coast. Other people in the car also lost their lives. I can't say any more about this for obvious reasons .We told our medium friend all about this as it all started to make sense now she had come back, and Barbara had the condition of how our friend had died put on her. Well he came to our home, we all said prayers for her, asked for her to be at peace and taken in to the light. Hopefully she is now at rest. On another occasion Barbara was up the stairs when she heard a tune being whistled and she knew it was the same person who said Jezebel bong ,on the stairs some time before when she came down and told me about it I started to hear the tune being whistled ; I said I can hear it, I hummed the tune I could hear and it was the same tune she had heard up the stairs, it seemed to me to come from high up and about thirty feet in front of me; we never heard that tune again .Coming up to Christmas Barbara was in the front room putting the Christmas tree up with my young daughter Laura, I was in the back room, As she was putting things on the tree, she started to get the feeling she was being watched and this feeling got stronger and stronger. She also got the feeling that she had not got to turn round but Barbara being Barbara, she turned round and just a few feet away at the back of her a man stood there looking at her and her at him! He was about thirty years old, in a grey suit. He just stood there, and then he was gone. My daughter saw nothing, Barbara knew that the man knew that she could see him; I was still in the back room. We have had many such incidents in this house far too many to write down here, so I will finish with this incident. One day Barbara saw a man and a woman in the bathroom at the side of the toilet, both in their late sixties or later. This is going to sound silly, but this is how it was. I can only write down how it was even if it does sound silly! They were both sort of leaning, sort of over the toilet but looking away, like looking across the room at something; Barbara had a very strong feeling that they did not want her in this house. She don't know why but she felt this very strong resentment of her Barbara also knew that I and my children were in no danger, it was just her they did not want in this house Barbara had said this to me on many occasions that; she felt that something in the house did not want her there. Any way sometime after this Barbara was going to use the bathroom but before this my daughter Sarah had fallen asleep down stairs so I picked her up and carried her to bed. As I got to my daughter's bedroom door which was shut, the door just opened right up! It fully opened, on its own! So I could just walk straight in carrying my daughter without touching the door. I was amazed! It was like I was being helped; that's how I saw it; this door had been opened for me by someone or something unseen! I put my daughter to bed; Lee was in the next room on his computer. I went down stairs and told Barbara what had just happened. Anyway she went to the toilet, but was very uneasy all the time about using the bathroom because of the things that had happened previously, so I said I will come with you, I will just be at my bedroom door which was only a few feet away and my son Lee was just in the next room. I said to her again, don't lock the door! But she did; within a matter of a minute or so she was screaming again! I had to kick the door open. My son came running out his bedroom to see what a matter was. As I went in to the bathroom, Barbara stood there with her hands up to her face, crying, with blood running through her fingers from a half inch cut up the side of her eye. Her eye was swelling up; I pulled her out the bathroom and tried to stop the bleeding. She said someone or something had hit her hard, in the eye, but there was no one there; only her in the bathroom! I was really mad I walked in to the bathroom closed the door and said come on you b-----d cowards, do it to me, but nothing happened. It took me about an hour to calm Barbara down a little, I had stopped the eye from bleeding but it was by now very swollen and she was shaking, she insisted she wanted to go see the vicar who lived just down the road. I took her to the vicarage and to be quite honest, he was a waste of space; he did not want to know! He said come back tomorrow, He did not even let us in! Well, the next day Barbara phoned another vicar at the church, who she had known for many years, she said I will come to say prayers in the house, but then refused to come if our friend was going to be there our friend being a spirit medium. She gave us a choice, our medium friend or her. He had no problem with her being there, He was quite happy to work together but she said no, so we chose our friend to come and do a spirit rescue. Barbara and I participated in this work with him. My friend was very nervous as he had been advised by other mediums not to attempt it on his own and he was made aware how dangerous this sort of work can be, but years ago he had been through similar experiences in his own home and family before he became a medium so he wanted to help my family and myself , as he was given help years ago when he needed it . At this point, I will point out how dangerous this can be .The medium that removed a troublesome spirit, from his home had her own home smashed up before she was able to remove the spirit which she had removed from his home to her home. As I said Barbara and I participated in this with him, so he would not be on his own. I had undertaken this sort of work before, but it was the first time for Barbara and was very unnerving for her .My friend also picked up that there was a man and woman in the bathroom. No one had mentioned this to him and he also went on to say they did not want Barbara in the house. Some time prior to this we had a trance medium in who basically said the same thing, at one stage we had asked for the angels of mercy to step forward and remove these earth bound spirits. All of a sudden I felt like I was being choked, I could not breathe! I was coughing, my eyes were running, it just came on me in seconds then went from me as fast as it came. I could have been picking up the condition of the spirit. Anyway after all this Barbara would not come back in to the house, so I moved. As I said we all had things happen to us in this house, even my then three year old daughter, as something tried to come in to her! I had to grab hold of her, pull her away from the table and take her in to another room. I am not going to go in to this but it was very frightening at the time. The trance medium said there's something in this house that's not very nice and it doesn't want your partner in this house. On a couple of occasions my son Scott felt the physical side of things. One night he was a sleep in bed when he was woken up by being shaken very violently by an unseen force, this scared him a lot. On another occasion he was in the bathroom when he felt something run down is back; there were marks down is back and his back was wet with what appeared to be water. Another time he went in to the bathroom and water ran down is back from nowhere. Sounds incredible, but it did happen. I have had a lot of experiences over the years but can't begin to understand things like this. Remembering back to one evening when I was talking to Barbara about some of the things that had taken place in this house while we had been there, when she said a young lad is trying to come to her. She said he's trying to tell me something he has been murdered. Then she started saying all sorts of things. I told her to stop. She said "I can't he's telling me these things". So I said we will write it down what he's saying. I got pen and paper and she started writing things down very fast. I was getting concerned for her as she seemed to be half in a trance. I told her to stop. She would not or could not. I raised my voice to her and she stopped, but said, "He wants to tell me what happened; he's very scared of his uncle". I said ok, well write it all down then, but don't let him take over you. She started writing again at some speed and using words she would not use. She asked me what some of the things meant, she had spoke about. The long and the short of what she wrote is, this young man or lad was very scared and Barbara could feel his fear; in fact, at one point she had tears in her eyes. I did tell her to stop, but she said, "No he wants to tell me". She went on to say the lad was hiding in a barn behind bales of hay or straw; his uncle was looking for him, he said his mother was pregnant. His uncle had raped her and killed her with a scythe then killed him with the scythe as well, so he was hiding from his uncle who was looking for him. You would think it would all be over once death takes place, but it was like the young lad was reliving it over and over again! Anyway, I stopped her writing any more, as I was getting concerned about her. She said the young lad did not want her to go, there was a lot more to tell, but I said, "no", because at times she did not seem to be in proper control of the situation, so she stopped, much to her annoyance or his. I have often thought if this is why Barbara was not wanted in the house, because she was capable of finding out what happened there on that site before the house was built on Beauvale road. Could be hundreds of years back; that's just a theory, but something did not want Barbara in this house at any cost, so it might have been to prevent her finding out what happened there centuries ago. Whatever the truth may be, something dark and very sinister was in that house on Beauvale road Hucknall and MAY STILL BE THERE!

What is in the Air? by Roy Walters

These photographs were taken on the 16th of August 2009 .From the back garden of my partners home in Hucknall I have taken a lot of photographs of orbs and mist from this location and holding true to form, the orbs were coming thick and fast. Some of the orbs I could see with my eyes so I knew where and when to take most of the photographs. Then I saw something small and silver in the air, it caught my eye as it sort of twinkled. I pointed my camera at it and took a photograph. It I was very surprised when I saw it, as it was nothing like the orbs I had been photographing. As I said, it was small in size but still large enough to see with your eyes. I was also surprised that it was still there in the air when I had taken the photograph. It had not gone, as most orbs do, so I quickly took another photo and it was still there! but seemed to be slowly moving .All in all, I was able to take a good dozen photographs or so and as you can see from the photographs, it is at different heights and is moving up the garden and goes in to a tree at the top of the garden and at one point seems to attach its self to the top of the outhouse roof. When I first saw it I would say it was about twenty to thirty feet up in the air. When it went in to the tree at the top of the garden, I was about fifty feet away, then. The photographs that are larger and closer I have zoomed in to the smaller photographs to show them in more detail and as you can see, they appear to be some kind of tube which looks like they have orbs inside them and appear to be shooting orbs out from both ends of it; or is it that orbs are just around them? I don't know. Whatever the case may be, I have never seen or photographed anything like it before. Clearly it is something small floating about in the, but what? And it also raises another question- is it harmful to the human race? As things in the air we tend to breathe in.

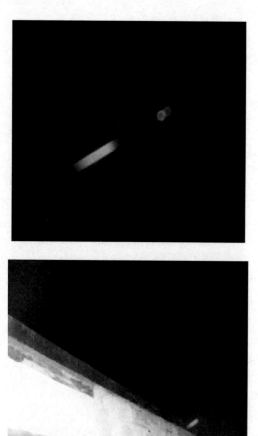

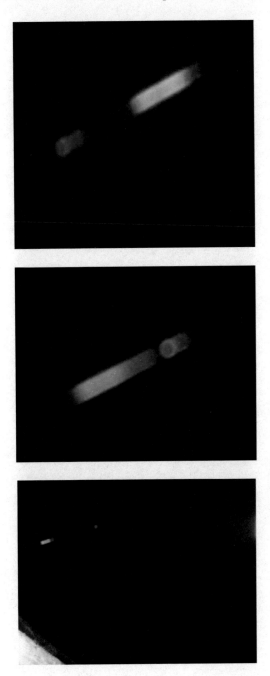

Feeling Time by Roy Walters

One day I was out walking around Hucknall cemetery, the one on Titchfield Park. I find cemeteries very relaxing and peaceful places and often have a walk round and read what is on the old grave stones from time to time. I also have quite a few family members and friends in this cemetery. Just down the side of the little old chapel there are some very old graves. I was walking down the side of this part stopping and reading what was on the grave stones .I came to one particular grave and as I was reading what was on the head stone, For a matter of only a few seconds , I felt the oldness of time .I WAS THERE IN THE 1800s ! I FELT IT. It was very weird, very serene. I DID NOT SEE ANYTHING IN THE 1800s, but I felt the 1800s. With every fibre of my body .Very hard to explain, But I felt the oldness of time .It had a warm, musky, safe feeling. A feeling you would want to hold on to for an entire life time. The next second I was just looking at a cold grave stone; the warm serene feeling the oldness had gone. I walked away, but felt depleted so I turned round and walked back, but just could not remember which grave it was .I couldn't understand it. One minute it was there, the next it's gone! Like it was never there. I could not feel anything. I've been down there many a time since to try and get that same feeling again. BUT NOTHING!.Why I felt it the first time and not after- wards I don't know .I have since thought ,perhaps I picked up the vibrations from the old grave stone , Or did I pick up the feelings and thoughts of the old couple in the grave? . Whichever it was, it was a very warm, calm, peaceful feeling. It was the pinnacle of serenity. And how it was to feel the 1800s! Words alone do not do it justice.To explain it, I may have just felt the peacefulness of the old couple and the time that they lived in. Whatever the case may be, I have never in my life felt as peaceful, safe, and happy as I did in those few short seconds at that grave side!

Visitation by Ernest Walters

This particular incident occurred at the military hospital at Colchester, Essex in 1962, late in the year, whilst I was stationed at the local Army Barracks there, serving in the Royal Green Jackets. It was not long after I had been home on leave for a few days whilst the family still resided at Padley Hall. The accident preceding my admittance to hospital that particular day occurred on the shooting ranges. I remember it was my turn for a day on the rifle ranges doing some butt marking, where we had to work the hand frames up and down with the targets in . As they worked on a pulley system, it wasn't difficult work and consequently a person's mind could wander. Of course , there was the usual amount of horse- play in between 'practices', which in fact really did very little to relieve the almost suffocating monotony of this dreadful annual chore . I remember my platoon sergeant once remarking to me that two of the dreaded chores in the Army were, Butt marking and changing 'denim buttons with the wirings. This particular day of the accident I was for some reason, wearing an anorak with a zip – pocket across the front of it and this was the cause of my hospital jaunt and consequent story. As I said, the target frames worked on a pulley system; as one frame was pushed up the other one came down. Whilst I was pushing up the frame a part of it caught in the flap pocket on the front of my anorak and pulled me in to the middle! Of course the back frame was coming down at the same time and I was consequently sandwiched between the two, resulting in some very severe pain and I was quiet dazed. It all happened so quickly that no one else seemed to notice. The firing was still in progress and rounds were still thudding into the bank about ten yards to our front! In sheer panic I took the most stupid course of action possible; I managed to extricate myself from the frames, but instead of falling back under the overhead shelter I ran forward still holding my stomach, towards the bank where the rounds were falling! Luckily, I collapsed at the bottom of it. Apparently someone must have thought I had been shot , as the ambulance arrived less than fifteen minutes after the accident and I was admitted to the Military Hospital at Colchester and then duly probed and prodded for the next twenty minutes be- for being bedded down for three days, for observation. I was then informed as to how lucky I was not to have taken the last volley in the back! Another couple of yards and I would have looked like one of their colanders, not just full of holes but bullet holes! The accident had occurred about mid-day and it was now about two thirty, so after being told to get some sleep I was left to my own devices for a couple of hours. At my second attempt at full consciousness, I perceived tea was in progress , but being by now almost famished, I thought I must be dreaming and I dozed off again , probably wouldn't have got any , anyway . I was awakened by a nurse at seven-thirty pm. and given a slice of bread and butter and a little fruit in syrup plus two white capsules, to help me sleep, then after paying my first visit to the toilet. I was left to get on with the nodding. Everywhere was so deathly quiet and still, not even any snorers or sleep walkers on the loose.The night nurse wasn't on duty yet, so it must still have been be- for ten o' clock. Eventually she came in and toured the ward. I pretended to be a-sleep then she came and sat down at the desk and sorted through a few papers. After about ten minutes she did another quick tour then left, switching the lights off on her way out. The ward was in almost complete darkness now, no snoring and almost as quiet as the grave. I could even hear my own breathing and the slight thump of my heart as the pulses seemed to accelerate slightly. This was the moment it began! At least I believe it all began at that moment , but looking back on it especially in the cold light of years instead of days I find it very difficult to pin point a beginning or even to know what the beginning was! I remember feeling a little nervous and uneasy, probably due to delayed shock. I tried to relax and sleep. The first sensation was a slight quivering of the lower –back muscles and then a tingling sensation all over my body; rather like pins and needles. Now I could feel the cold coming on; not icy, just cold and I began to shiver slightly, even though I knew I was slightly wet with perspiration. I felt a sort of prickly' sensation over the top of my head and at the back of my neck. Even though the thought crossed my mind that this was just imagination or hallucination , I knew intuitively what was taking place, as this was, indeed , not the first time I had been through some similar experiences in my life !. I forced myself to open my eyes, expecting to see nothing and having this confirmed. Now I felt this almost familiar, intangible, yet somehow very concrete force pressing very lightly on the lower half of my legs ; almost as if someone were sitting on them! . The pressure on the legs continued for a few minutes, and then moved up the body towards the chest. I was not unduly concerned at this stage, as this had been previously fairly familiar territory but then the pressure started to increase rather rapidly. The very atmosphere around me now felt quite ominously alive with some form of nameless, malevolent entity! I tried to raise my arms to push away the bedclothes, but found to my horror that I could not lift them one inch! I felt just as if I was embedded in a solid block of concrete, which was slowly trying to crush the very life from me! I was absolutely paralysed from the neck down now. I became almost hysterical and at a complete loss as to what to do next. The pressure on my chest was still slowly increasing and I could discern a sort of pulsating motion, over my entire body, yet above it and travelling up and down. Who's there? I whispered softly! Not really expecting to receive any reply. Again I asked much louder and more desperately this time, who's there? What do you want? No reply of any description and after a slight pause I murmured, go away, go away, several times. In some past experiences of this nature this had usually worked and whatever the force / Entity was, it had departed within a short time. Not this time! Oh no, it wasn't going to just disappear this time, Now I thought I was in for a fight; a fight to the death; mine! This force or Entity or whatever it is very difficult to describe to anyone who has not had any similar experience. It is something – Evil, which is there and at the same time, not there. I suppose the nearest experience to it would be something like a nervous breakdown, first my head and then the whole ward began to spin, faster and faster, as if I were extremely intoxicated or caught up in a cyclone, being whirled to the centre and final oblivion. My body was being pressed deeper and deeper in to the mattress, until I felt as if I were being sucked in to a bottomless black well or tunnel and at the same time being pushed from above. Hold on, hold on, I was chanting, over and over and still being whirled almost in to Eternity. I thought that someone or something was trying to suck the soul out of my body and send it right to Hell! I'm going limp, I can't hold on much longer! The thoughts were racing through my brain! I opened hysterical, terror- filled eyes, searching desperately for the night nurse, who was not there. Pray, that's it pray, shout for the night nurse, anyone, my brain was screaming, Nurse, but nothing came from my throat, not a whisper, I tried again and again and again, but no sound came out . Now I knew I was on my own; my whole existence depended entirely on my, weak defenceless will. Perhaps it was, after all, just my imagination gone wild, perhaps I had lost my reason was going mad. By hell! I wished it was true! I wished I was going mad, because if not I could be dead! The pressure was now almost unbearable and I was having great difficulty in breathing properly. I don't know to this day , how or why or to whom I was praying, or to what, but I was really praying ; for ; for real ; for me ! The ward lights suddenly snapped on and I tried to scream again for the nurse, but in vain. Then I saw her entering the ward, she was half a mile away and seemed to be floating along as if in a slow motion film. She did not take the slightest notice of me and eventually disappeared behind a set of screens at the far end of the ward. I kept on praying and thinking of the colour blue, everything blue and peaceful then I started to think of a crucifix, and as I thought harder , it seemed to grow and stretch its self over the length of the bed, glowing a sort of bluish brilliant white. My survival instinct must have been much stronger than my will- power, as I am still here today. Then someone was shaking my arm and calling me by my first name. The blonde grey hair and fresh features of a sister floated before my eyes and my first thought was that I was in a mental home. I jumped up sharply and instantly recognised my own ward which seemed almost flooded with light, and the night nurse was accompanied by an orderly on the other side of the bed. The sister asked what was wrong with me, telling me that they had spent ten minutes trying to bring me round and that my sheets and I were wet through with perspiration. I replied that I must have had a bad dream. The sister seemed to accept this explanation for the time being and had me transferred after a quick wipe down and change of night wear to a vacant bed on the other side almost opposite my own. Before leaving, the night nurse told me to try and get some sleep and not to worry. I glanced over to my own bed and immediately felt my scalp prickle, as I noticed some broken metal structure hanging down under the bed, then I felt a cold grip of terror again, as I looked at the bed legs and saw that all four seemed to be somehow embedded in to the wooden floor or the wood had been indented. Pulling the blankets up over my head I thought I am all right now any way they have left the lights on. As I was falling asleep it struck me that I would be required to give a fuller explanation the following morning. It also struck me that it seemed only by some incomprehensible intervention that I would still be around to give that explanation.

Goodbye Was In the Air by Roy Walters

This incident took place, while I was living on Beauvale road in Hucknall. For a couple of weeks or so, I and Barbara were visiting her uncle in city hospital, Nottingham. He had been ill for a while, and we were usually down there at tea time visiting. One afternoon, Barbara came over exceptionally tired, for no apparent reason, and decided not to go to the hospital that day, but said we will go tomorrow instead. So with that I decided to do a cooked dinner for tea. I was in the kitchen cooking all windows and doors were shut, the oven was on and all four gas rings were on. It was extremely hot in the kitchen, then from nowhere, I had an icy blast of cold air hit me full in the face, as refreshing as it was, I could not understand where it had come from. It was like opening a freezer door, and sticking your head in it. Icy cold straight in your face, then gone in a matter of a couple of seconds. I looked at the clock on the kitchen wall, 5 30 pm it was tea time, I went in to the living room and told Barbara, what had just taken place, and told her to note the time, because from past experience of strange things just happening, I knew it was for a reason that would be revealed at a later stage, which I was proved to be right. You don't get a freezing cold blast of air in your face in a red hot kitchen from nowhere without a reason. Any way we had our tea, and then I took Barbara over to her house. Round about 8. 30 pm. or so that evening ,Barbara's two cousins came to her home , to tell her that their father , Barbara's uncle had just died a few hours earlier about 5.30pm. If we had a gone to the hospital that day, we would have been sitting with him instead of his son when he passed. Obviously ,and its only my opinion, but I strongly believe events were put in to place paranormally ,to prevent Barbara and myself being with him when he passed ,in preference to his son, being with him . And the time, 5.30pm. Obviously again he let us know, of his passing you could say just coincidence, but I think not but having said that you make your own mind up.

Premonition by Roy Walters

A few short years ago, I was coming out a shop on Annesly road Hucknall . With my partner Barbara. We saw two of Barbara's relatives, and both of them being pregnant. They were standing there chatting away about their condition, as pregnant ladies do. I was not taking much notice , well men don't do they, and I sort of lost myself in my own thoughts, just sort of ,day dreaming ,I suppose . When my attention, was brought sharply back, to them all talking about babies. And I got the most horrible feeling, a very deep knowing, that only one baby would be born. I looked at them both, but did not know which one of them would give birth, and who would not. But I did know without a shadow of a doubt, that one of them was going to lose their baby. A knowing, from deep inside. I said nothing how could I? I was in a bit of a predicament, to say the least. Some four weeks or so went by, and my partner Barbara, heard the sad news of the miscarriage. Not a nice thing to see before it happens, but happen it did. I have had to leave all names out for obvious reasons. These sorts of things must bring thoughts in to all our minds. Is our life planed out for us, yes I think it is. I believe three quarters of what happens in our life is pre-set for us. If someone sees something happen, before it happens, well to me that's impossible, but I've seen lots of things, that's happened a short time after. In one case just a minute, then I stood there and watched happen, what I had just seen happen, a minute, prior to this. The point is, how you can see something happen before it does, it must be set out to happen. I have seen people die, sometimes at their time of death, told people about it, only to have it confirmed later. I think the biggest part of our life is pre-set out for us, which in my eyes makes us just like pawns, in a game of chess. Sometimes, very strange things happen to change events, to put you in a certain, place at a certain time, or even to remove you , from what is about to take place, so you are not party to it . Things are not just coincidence, they are pre- set to happen, make no mistake about that.

Friendly Visitor by Roy Walters

Round about 1998, I moved in to a council flat on the out skirts of Hucknall ,for a year or so

Whilst in this flat we did experience spirit activity.

When I say we, I mean myself, my partner Barbara, and my young son Scott.

Who was then round about nine years old.

Shortly after we moved in to the flat We became aware that we were not alone.

I think Barbara was the first to see the spirit of a youngish woman round about forty to forty five years old; she was dressed as they would have done in the early 1800s.

There was nothing threatening or unpleasant about her, she was just there.

The reason for her being there we don't know, most probably there was no reason at all.

From time to time if you're a little sensitive to spirit, some time you will see them other times you may feel them, or even hear them, there don't have to be a reason.

Spirit is around us all the time, but most of the time, you're not aware of them, as we are too busy with everyday life.

Noise is very hard to get away from, if you turn everything off and try and sit quietly for a while and relax, sort of let your mind go in to a sort of day dream mode, these are the times if your sensitive to spirit, when you might become aware of them around you, or around your home, and I also say this to you spirit don't just come at night, they are there all the time, I have seen and been aware of spirit day time, afternoon, in the night, in the morning, just about any time of day .

I reflect back on the time when my son Scott, woke up and there was a woman sitting on the bottom of his bed reading a book, this was in the flat.

It may have been the same lady Barbara saw, Scott said she was an old woman, but at nine years old I suppose to him someone in their middle forties would be old, someone of that age a child would see as old.

Scott says she scared him, but I think he just got a bit of a shock, which is understandable under the circumstances, but I don't think there was any intension to scare him, any way she did not even seem aware of him.

Scott is now a lot older and has seen spirit quite a few times, and he has also heard spirit speak to him, but he still gets scared.

One evening myself Alan and a group of friends ,did a paranormal investigation at the bowman Hotel in Hucknall ,to which my son Scott ,sat in with us, and he was aware of spirit around us that evening and also at a house on Bolsover Street in Hucknall, where Alan and I investigated the property .

Getting back to the flat, one evening I had just got in to bed ,my two sons Lee and Scott, was already in bed ,all of a sudden it was like all of my senses where up, a young woman stepped in to the door way of my bedroom ,and I got the feeling and words in my head just checking, then she was gone and this is something, I cannot explain properly but I saw her, but I did not see her ,an explanation is too hard to put in to words how it was .

Another time I had just got in to bed, Lee and Scott were in bed in their room, Barbara was knocking about in the kitchen, I could hear her but could not see her.

Then I felt movement on the bed ,as if someone had pressed themselves up to me, I felt no fear at all, I can't even say if they were on the bed ,or in the bed, I just don't know ,then Barbara walked to the bed room door, and it just moved away from me, but as Barbara went back in to the living room it came back and pressed up against me again, and I felt the bed move, well not really the bed ,but the mattress around me, Barbara came back to say something again, and it went and did not come back .

Another, time I was in the passage of the flat, and I felt a small dog run round and in-between my legs, I did not see or hear anything but I certainly felt it.

Another incident that happened in the flat, Barbara and I had fallen out, and she had gone back home.

I went to bed straight away, I was aware of a woman at the side of my bed ,and I felt she was very annoyed with me not angry, but annoyed, because of the argument with Barbara, I just knew all this it was like it was placed in my head ,the next thing a small dog was placed on my chest, I could feel its little feet but could see nothing, I put my hands together as if to grab it, but got the feeling of dry sand running through my fingers, then the dog was gone, also the woman ,it felt like the dog had dissolved, I know all this happened because I had fallen out with Barbara, and that is why the woman was annoyed with me, who she was I don't know .

After this I never heard, felt or was aware of this woman again, and neither was Barbara.

The Bowman by Roy Walters

I and a group of friends went along to the Bowman Hotel Hucknall last year 2009.

At the request of the manager and staff.

To do a paranormal investigation in to spirit activity, that had been taking place over a long period of time.

A certain member of staff who resided at the Bowman, was being woken up in the night by being rigorously shaken, also he had seen on more than one occasion a lady sitting on the bottom of his bed in the night giving him restless nights.

Also things occasionally flew off the shelves in the kitchen area ,and at one point a knife was torn from some ones hand ,and members of staff being slightly pushed in the back I experienced this myself in the kitchen area .

A few hours before undertaking the investigation, I sat in meditation at home

In my mind I placed myself in the function room upstairs of the Bowman, and within a few minutes, I saw an old lady standing in front of me in the middle of the function room.

I would say this lady appeared to be in her seventies, grey hair tied back in a tight bun at the back of her head, she was of medium build and average height, and she just stood looking at me.

I calmly said hello what's your name? to which I received no reply just a sort of blank steer in a few seconds she was gone.

A little later that evening, I met my friends at the Bowman along with my son Scott, who participated in the investigation that evening.

As things got underway in a small room just off from the function room, the atmosphere in this part felt very heavy and oppressive, it felt like I was buckling at the knees and felt like I was swaying .

Alan and Christan felt very much the same infac't it had a feeling of someone being hung there so we said some prayers and asked for this area to be cleared of all negative energies.

Within a minute the area felt a lot better even warmer and lighter.

One could say just imagination well that matters not

has we believe in what we do and if we made a difference to someone or something struggling to pass over properly for whatever reason ,then to us it is well worth our time and effort .

What really matters is this we full heartedly believe in what we do.

As the evening progressed Alan picked up an old lady in the middle of the function room , at this point I had not mentioned to anyone what I picked up only hours earlier, that being the old lady, so that was conformation to me .

Alan then felt the presence of a young child a girl, who was crying about five years old so with this we placed a circle of chairs round and formed a circle.

Round about this time, I felt the old lady at the back of me just watching

So at this point I got up and started taking photographs as you can see from the photograph .

There is an orb inside the circle and another two orbs outside the circle, and of course the empty seat where I had previously been sitting.

A little later that evening Carol a member of our little group went in to the ladies toilet.

Whilst in there she heard a lady crying in distress ,then she distinctly heard a man's voice angrily saying, get out this was directed at carol.

Alan and I moved to the kitchen area and once again I got this swaying and tilting feeling, then I was pushed lightly in my back, it did not appear to be threatening, it was more like yes I am here.

We did not really experience much more in there.

On talking to the manager, a little later that evening, he was telling us about feeling someone walk right past him in the bar area, but he could see no one and there were times when he says he has felt some one right behind him at the back of the bar, when there was only himself there a little sheepishly he said he quickly locked up and left .

He also told us about one evening when he was at the back of the bar someone opened the door and walked in then closed the door and walk towards him , but there was no one there .

He seemed to be getting more nervous by the minute so I pulled his leg a little.

Anyway I presume he had a good night's sleep .

From my information I hear that spirit continues to be active from time to time at the Bowman.

I know they used to have quite a few clairvoyant evenings in the function room don't know if this has any bearing on anything could do I suppose .

I know there are plenty of spirits at the back of the bar.

Paranormal Linby (Written by Alan Smith)

About 10 miles out of the metropolis that is Nottingham City Centre lies a rather quiet, leafy village, where visitors to the area can enjoy a leisurely walk around this ancient village that was once adjoined to the great Sherwood Forest, maybe taking in a drink at the local hostelry which stands as a focal point on the main road, or maybe taking a look inside the 13th century church of St. Michael which was probably built in the late part of the 12th century, possibly on the site of the church hinted at in the Doomsday book of 1086, but does the quiet façade of this ancient village hide more than it is prepared to allow its visitors to witness? Could this timeless village be home in fact to a great range of paranormal activity?

On land which borders the two villages of Linby and Papplewick lie the hidden foundations of long demolished mills, mills where, in the 18th and early 19th centuries, great numbers of pauper children were employed, these children having been 'imported' from the London workhouses. These children, who were drafted into industry to save public expense as they were deemed cheap labour, suffered terribly from the industrial conditions of the age, having to work long hours, being badly fed and clothed, in addition to being poorly housed. As a result of this treatment, many children died and were laid to rest in the churchyards, mainly in unmarked graves, and not always entered in the church Registers. One authority places the number in Linby Church¬yard alone at one hundred and sixty three – although the church registers record just forty two.

Linby is, in its own rights, a village that gives credence to reputed paranormal activity, for despite it's location on a busy road, it is a 'quiet' village, and as one walks through the village, one cannot fail to sense or recognise the air of days gone by. The village has several reputed locations, but being ever the intrepid, we set our sights on a particular piece of land which we have been led to believe to be 'common land' – paranormally active common land that is!

The land of which we talk is roughly triangular in shape, is edged on one side by a public pathway, while the Linby – Papplewick main road runs by on the other. So it was then, that with having had that one particular area of the 'Paranormal Linby' pointed out to us, we decided to see for ourselves just what might possibly lay hidden in the long forgotten, dusty, historic pages of this village, pages that makes this village so paranormally active.

Do the souls of the long forgotten children still roam the area of the mills today? Who or what else lurks in the hedgerows and lanes of this village, maybe soldiers from the 12th century (or earlier) Annesley Fort, or maybe there are16th century soldiers from the time of King Charles still patrolling this area?

During the hours of daylight, the land of which we talk is quite unassuming, but when darkness starts to descend, an ethereal presence soon prevails, and an eerie coolness settles quickly and quietly upon its terrain. Is it's history about to be revealed to those who seek the truth of what lies beneath the light of day and beyond all 'normal' senses, it certainly exudes an aura of expectancy, so, with an open mind, let us now investigate this part of 'Paranormal Linby'.

Having seen several atmospheric (i.e. eerie) photographs that Nottingham Paranormal Network (NPN) had previously taken in this area, we could not help but be impressed by what we saw, from mists that are there one second and literally gone the next second, mists that are invisible to the naked eye, mists in which can be discerned shapes/faces/animals – it depends how you look at them (try looking at the photographs from several angles), and as for the number of 'Orb' photo's, well these are more than substantial to say the least.

Orbs - sphere's of light - are frequently dismissed as being anything other than naturally occurring phenomena, and even as believers in the spirit world, there have been many times when we have doubted the authenticity of some photographs we've seen, nevertheless, we hope the accompanying photographs allow you to see for yourself that orbs are not always of this dimension.

No matter just exactly what Orbs are, It is not possible - in words - for us to prove to you just how intelligent Orbs are, this is something you would have to experience for yourself, but with this type of phenomena being somewhat prevalent within this locality, we will endeavour to show you that not all Orbs are rain drops, insects, Chinese lanterns etc - as the following photographs will hopefully illustrate.

As can be seen in the below, an insect is clearly visible flying through the darkness while orbs of light can be plainly seen in the background, so this (to us) debunks the idea that all Orbs are insects, for that obviously just isn't so.

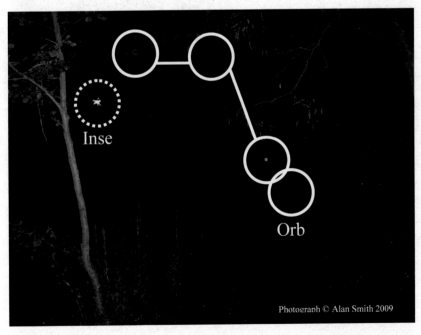

Photograph © Alan Smith 2009

I say that Orbs have an intelligence because of our experience of them, I've lost count of the number of times I've said "I've got something round me right now" only for Roy to take a photograph and capture a spherical light - an Orb - either around me or moving away from me.

Below is an example of what I mean; I had sensed 'something' around me, and Roy had actually and physically seen an Orb near me, so with a swift click of the camera button Roy captured the Orbs you can see above me and in front of me. These Orbs actually stayed with us for sometime as Roy and I walked along the path shown, they were photographed several times around me as we walked.

Photograph © Roy Walters

Neither Roy or I are scientists, so we are unable to offer any explanation as to just exactly what Orbs are, but no matter what they are, Spirit forms or otherwise, what you can see is not something that 'appears' to be a solid form, for so many – but not all - Orbs are quite translucent. The one thing that many people do agree on is the fact that Orbs are energy of some sort, but quite what that energy is, or from where that energy originates, remains a mystery.

Intelligent Orbs = intelligent energy, the two statements just have to go together, and if the energy is intelligent, then Orbs cannot be of this dimension, for where on Earth can intelligent energy like this be found - and be found willing to 'work' with people who are spiritually aware.

An example of Orb's willingness to work with people, or be around people, can be seen in the following images. An Orb had been captured by Roy 'floating' round a bench seat, so by way of experiment I sat down on the bench and began 'asking out' for our

Spirit friend to come and be near me, and as can be seen below, this is exactly what happened.

Orb's however are not confined to just one place, they're a growing worldwide phenomena, more and more frequently captured thanks to the everyday use of digital cameras. However, some places seem more 'active' with them than others, this ranges from houses to churches, to back gardens, to fields, and even circuses, yet why such a field as the one we're investigating here be so active? I wouldn't like to say for certain, but given the local history of the area (see above), it feeds the mind enough to make one wonder if these are the Spirits of those who are long departed from this earth.

The following few photographs display several Orbs in different varieties!

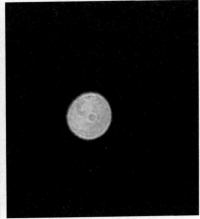

We have one photograph in our collection that both Roy and myself are very proud off, in fact we feel privileged to have captured such an Orb on camera, and it wasn't captured just once, we've actually 'caught it' on several photographs.

The photograph itself is included below, but before we present it to you, and despite what might be said about photograph manipulation, I can assure readers that none of the photographs in this article have been manipulated in any way – with the exception of enlarging sections of photographs in order to show in more detail the Orbs posted above or to brighten/darken the image.

As I say, the photograph you are about to see is one that most people find really interesting, and until the moment I saw it for the first time, I would never have thought it possible for a Orb to look like the one posted below:

An Orb with a great big smiley face, and an image of a Spirit person in the bushes behind me, now personally I find this photograph amazing, and while the Spirit person appears to be missing in other photographs we took that evening, the smiley face can be seen in several other photographs - and in other locations, including being above me again when we were on the main road back into Linby village.

Where then do these Orbs come from, it's easy enough to say 'out the sky', but here again Roy and I have been given an insight as to their possible means of transportation, mass transportation – Mists.

Mists

Until I walked across this field for the first time in the company of the co-founders of NPN, I had never heard of the phenomena of Spirit mists, nor had I ever seen one, so I was amazed to see such phenomena captured by camera in front of my own eyes. Now despite the way in which I have written the above paragraph, these mists are not (as far as I'm aware) visible to the naked eye, but the digital camera captures them very well as you shall soon see.

Above I stated that mass Orb transportation 'can be made' by Mists, and this is something both Roy and I have both come to accept as 'a' definite - though not definitive - means of Orb transportation, for it cannot be pure coincidence that the 'appearance' of one of these mists creates a massive trail of Orbs.

Below is one example of the Mists I talk of, where do they come from?

Well, we have captured them with wispy tails emanating from the earth itself, but whether or not these 'wispy tails' are actually leaving the earth or indeed entering it, I have no idea, but the amazing thing is that they should be photographed at all.

In the above photograph, a solitary Orb can be seen just under the wispy letter 'd' in the top left quadrant of the picture, moments later, the Mist had disappeared but it had left behind (as can be seen in the photograph below) a mass of Orb phenomena. The more Roy and I amble across this particular area, the more questions we seem to be faced with, and the Mist connection with the Orbs is just one more question we would like answering.

Mass Orbs (post Mist)

Surprising to see so many Orbs in one image isn't it? And yet every time we capture a mist, we capture a mass of Orb phenomena in the air literally seconds after the mist. We can't explain what occurs - or the science behind it, but we're willing to learn in order that we may be able to pass on any conclusions sent to us – especially those conclusions from the scientific boffins.

Posted here is the first Mist photograph I ever witnessed being taken, and it is posted here courtesy of Mr Kristian Lander from NPN as is the picture beneath it.

I wrote earlier about Mists leaving or entering the earth, and on the photograph below is an example of a Mist, but is it leaving the earth or entering it?

Included in this section is another photograph, that we would like to show you, it doesn't really look like a Mist, but its very presence is worthy of note given the subject matter being written about.

Just what it is I've no idea, it's an amazing photograph, but look closely into the brightness of the 'Mist', what do you see?

Did you see anything in it? – Well let's rotate it 180o and see what you see then:

I showed this photograph to one person, her reaction was "If I didn't believe in extra terrestrials before seeing this, I believe in them now", and having looked at it several times since, I can see what she means, for there does appear to be a small (maybe 'baby') alien laying like a foetus in a mothers womb – complete with umbilical cord going into (or out of) the bushes. Spooky!

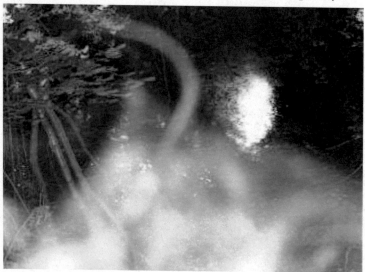

Other Phenomenon

As is implied, other additional phenomenon has been experienced, though no photographs are currently in our photographic library to support or substantiate the following.

1: Blue!

The very first time I field walked this particular area with Kristian and Sylvia (from NPN) it was a dark but warm evening, and we were privileged to witness a blue aura emanating from the ground about 100 yards in front of us, it was stunning to see such a thing happen, and I just couldn't help but wonder what it was – and I'm still no nearer knowing!

If you look at the photograph above taken in the tunnel of bushes, you'll be able to appreciate what I'm about to relate to you. It was during the above same walk that a distinct (very bright, very intense) blue light could be seen literally shining through the tunnel of bushes; it was almost as if a giant torch was being shone into the tunnel from behind the tree's and bushes for we could see the branches of the trees and bushes in front of the light, and to be honest it was extremely scary to witness it. I couldn't go near it, it 'felt' bad, in fact, the closest we went to it was about 100 to 150 yards, and the fact that a shadowy figure could be seen in the light... well, I'll leave you to guess how unsettled we felt.

2: Big Bird!

There is a public pathway which runs alongside 'the' field, it leads to from Linby to the adjoining village of Papplewick, and its route takes you close by St James Church (Papplewick), and this church has always been a taboo location for us, for we do have respect for the resting place of those passed to Spirit.

The time after the one in which we experienced the blue light, we were approaching the end of the field where the tunnel of bushes is, wondering if we would see said light again, or if we'd 'feel safe' to walk through this tunnel', the answer we sought was shown to us in a far different manner than our earlier visit, for both Kristian and I witnessed a giant black bird flying through the night sky, circling a big tree, and actually landing in the said tree whereupon it disappeared only to be see a few seconds later circling in the sky once again.

How would you know if it actually landed in the tree or not, for surely you wouldn't have been able to see do so because of the foliage? Ordinarily I'd agree with you, but it was an autumn/winter evening and there was no foliage whatsoever on the tree – hence our clear and uninterrupted view of where the 'bird' went.

We took that as a very definite warning not to proceed any further, now that might well make us sound frightened, and yes it was somewhat unsettling, but when a person is spiritually aware, one gets certain feelings/vibrations, and you soon learn to trust them. It's an easy rule to follow; take heed and keep safe, for while Spirits are 'reputedly' unable to hurt people, believe me friend, this is not always the rule – and we weren't taking any chances!

3: AVP (Actual Voice Phenomena)

To date we have only heard one instance of AVP, and that was one summers evening during 2009. It was a light but cool evening, and as we walked (Roy and I that is) we heard the unmistakeable sound of a young girl happily humming to herself. It took us a few seconds to realise just what we'd heard, and so we asked out for whoever it was who'd hummed to hum again, but we never heard it again. We couldn't see anyone, there was no rustling of leaves or snapping of twigs on the floor as if someone was moving around, and there was definitely no tittering as if someone had found it funny that we should be asking out, nothing!

Having said that, we did take a couple of photographs in that particular area, and one of them we managed to capture a distinct Blue Orb, and this is shown in the Orb phenomena section above.

Could this humming have been the sound of a Spirit girl from times gone by, we believe so, but we've no proof.

4: Hedgerow

The last instance of phenomena we'd like to record here is the mysterious golden light that was captured in the hedgerow of 'the field' during the summer of 2009.

The light of which I talk was captured by Roy one June evening when he and a few friends went along to see if they might capture anything paranormal on film.

This was not the only 'light' captured that evening, for another golden light was captured in the sky two or three minutes later, and this was duly submitted to our local newspaper who ran it as 'UFO caught on camera'. It is of interest to note that the position of the light in the sky is more or less exactly above where the light in the hedge was photographed – compare the position of it using the top of the hedgerow as a guide.

Returning to the picture of the light in the hedge, Roy submitted this photograph to a group called 'Association for the Scientific Study of Anomalous Phenomena' (ASSAP), their verdict? A glow worm!

Continuation of Paranormal Linby and Other Phenomenon by Roy Walters

A SSAP, state and I quote, the light that is in the bushes is a fascinating photo as the object is yellow , implying it is not a reflection of camera flash, and it appears to be in or behind a bush .They also state it appears to be in two parts obviously, it is some kind of glowing object . They also go on to say, that it could well be a very rare photo, of a glow worm. Well a glow worm I think not. This photograph was taken on the 27th June 2009 time 9-40 pm. when I took this photograph I never noticed the light in the bushes. I took the photograph, of my brother Richard,and a friend setting up their camera, the object of this was to see if I could photograph any orbs around them. A few moments later, I walked down the field a little way and then took another photograph, but this time I saw a large ball of white light in the sky above the tree tops, which I had captured on camera. I said to my brother Richard, what the hell is that? we had no idea, and within seconds it had gone Putting my photos on computer later that evening, I noticed the light in the bushes, the photos are numbered , and the bright ball of light in the sky was taken just a few moments later putting these two photographs together, it transpires that the light in the sky, is more or less directly above where the light in the bushes where . It is my believe, that these are in some way connected, I don't know. But for both the light in the bushes and the light in the sky to be present within a few moments of each other, and in the same location , both unexplained and let's face it they should not have been there at all , you could say just coincidence well I for one don't believe in coincidence . Note the light in the bushes is very intense light, look at the photo I have zoomed in to.

Obviously the light in the bushes is not the same as the light in the sky, as this is much bigger and more intense, BUT considers this is it possible that the light in the bushes actually went up in to the light in the sky. It certainly is possible. And again where did both lights go.

It also transpires that later that evening just a mile away a very bright zigzagging light was seen in the sky by a Mr Desmond turner, of Ruffs Estate Hucknall something he had never seen before, and certainly could not explain then or now .

Light in Bushes and Sky by Roy Walters

These photographs were taken on the 27th of june 2009 location linby-papplewick photo 1 showes light in bushes photo 2 showes photo zoomed in photo 3 showes same photo zoomed right in a few minutes later there was a huge ball of intense light in the sky directly above where the light in the bushes had been shown on photo 4 photo 5 showes same but zoomed in to time photographs were taken 9 40 pm all photoes taken by Roy Walters

Strange Mist by Roy Walters

In June of this year 2010, Alan and I were out over Papplewick taking photographs.

We photographed many orbs, at various locations.

On our way home, Alan, suddenly became aware of what we took to be spirit presence, very close to us to our left side, with this feeling being very strong, Alan took a photograph.

We were both very surprised as to what was revealed on the photograph, as you can see below

It appears to be a very huge vortex of mist, which was not visible to the eye, the very next second it was gone, nothing on the next photograph, taken seconds later.

Ordinarily mist just rising from the ground, would not just end in a sharp defined circle, the mouth of a funnel.

You can see the misty funnel is very dense, surly it would also be visible to the eye, with it being so large and dense, and how can something as pronounced as this, be gone, in a matter of a second?

Having said that, we cannot honestly say, what it is, I cannot say to you ,yes this is spirit, we can only give you the facts, as they are, and that is, the very strange feeling one gets, when you just know someone, or something, is very close to you, take a photo, as we did, and that is what came out on the photograph, yet again we can only bounce the ball back to the reader , and say you decide yourself.

strange mist appears after spitit activity mist not visible to naked eye but caught on camera by roy walters on friday 23rd april 2010 time 10.15 pm .

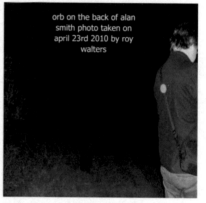

orb on the back of alan smith photo taken on april 23rd 2010 by roy walters

While out doing a paranormal investigation in the area of Linby and Papplewick with friends Alan and Julie .
spirit activity was picked up around us by Julie and Alan .
photographs were taken of many orbs that evening but at one point Julie sensed spirit around us and Alan picked up the name racheal to which he comented i have spirit around me now .
i said stand still i will take a photograph .
when i took the photograph it showes Alan surrounded by a thick mist which was not visible to the naked eye .
Another strange thing about this photograph is that the mist seems to be emiting from julies head and face conpleatly blanking her face out but you can clearly see Alan in the mist .
Itook another photograph two seconds later but the strange mist had gone.

Hauntings Worthing Sussex by Rosalind Hobbs

The long shadow of the past of this building, reaches far back in to time, and as worn many faces of change, right up till the present time, with events woven in to the very fabric of time. Events that occasionally resurface, and show their hand, on many occasions residents and staff alike, witnessed for them self's, the ghostly apparitions of yester year. The care home where I have worked for the past six years, goes right back to the early 1800s, and most probably a lot further back than that, as it has changed hands so many times .At one stage way back in to the distant past the home was a pig farm . And as the story goes, the old farmer who owned the land then, had a son called Jeffery; the farmer was renowned for his raging temper, and cruelty towards his son. At the age of eighteen ,this poor young man ,Jeffery hung himself, in what was then the loft where all the bales of hay were stored ,this now being one of our rooms upstairs ,see picture of beam where Jeffery is reputed to have taken his own life by hanging.

Jeffery spent most of his time up in the loft, away from his cruel father, and is still in the house to this very day, he stays upstairs and goes in to different rooms and talks to the residents, and sits there on their wardrobes. The residents tell us what he is wearing; they ALL describe the same person. One day last year ,2009 ,the cleaners were hoovering ,when all of a sudden, all the doors slammed shut ,and I felt a pressure on the left side of my face, and I know this might sound funny ,but he made a pig noise in my ear, it was rather scary and I came out the room very quickly, to say the least. On more than one occasion, he has touched my arm, when I have gone in to the loft, and no one likes to go up there alone. But there are times when we have to get supplies, but having said that, Jeffery as never harmed any one. There are other people here to, or should I say ghosts, spirits, whatever one wishes to call them. A young lady with a very nice voice often calls my name, but when I turn around there is no one there. Jimmy Edwards, who many will remember from the early sixties, from his comedy TV shows, his lovely wife Valarie was a resident here , one day I went to her room and she said to me , could that lady have a piece of paper ,so I said what lady ? She said the lady sitting at the end of my bed. She is showing you her shoe, she needs to clean the pigs mess off it. Valarie Edwards did not know that this home in the years gone by used to be a pig farm. On another occasion, sometime in May 2009, I saw an old lady through the window, at the rest Home. I watched her as she bent forward, and seemed to be picking something up off the floor, she had old brown trousers on ,and a green coat, she looked as if she had just come in off a farm ,this old lady has been seen on numerous occasions by other members of staff, and residents ,when I went in to the room there was no one there ,not long after this event ,I was up stairs at the rest home, as I looked up and towards an open door way, I saw a young coloured child about eight years old or so, she seemed to be playing in the door way, but had an angry expression on her face, I stood there in shock for maybe a minute or so, then she seemed to back up in to the room . I had a funny feeling that she knew I could see her ,then she was gone, she did not appear to be a happy child, and the very strange thing about all of this, is that I saw it all in black and white, like an old black and white photograph . What all that was about, I am clearly at a loss to give an explanation. I know I am very sensitive to spirit, as I have seen lots of spirit people in the home, but other members of staff have also seen the same things, and as I have already said, residents as well. On another occasion, when I was out driving in my car, I saw my late father sat in the back seat of the car, as I was going round an island, this gave me a big shock ,when I got round the island and pulled the car over, my father was no longer there . I have also seen my father, in my bedroom ,sitting on my bed with his back towards me, he then got up off the bed and walked right through the bedroom wall, he never spoke to me or tried any sort of communication ,apart from me seeing Him. At the later end of last year 2009, I was pottering about my home, when I saw a young woman walk down my stairs, for a split second I thought it was my daughter ,then the realisation dawned on me that it was not my daughter ,as I looked at her ,I was also aware that this young lady, was aware that I could see her , and vice versa , I was a little to shocked to say anything to her ,then she simply vanished , one moment she was there, the next she had gone . I know I share my home with many spirits, as I have seen them on many occasions, but I, or any of my family, has never been harmed by them. I suppose it's a bit like having an extended family around.

On the 31st of June 2010, I was at work with my colleague Maureen, we were down stairs in the passageway, generally talking about the young man that had hung himself from the beam picture above, my friend Maureen, started to feel very dizzy and sick.

Then I suddenly became aware of a spirit person, standing very close to me, on my left hand side

It was somewhat distressing, as it appeared the person had been in a fire, as it was black.

Also it appeared to have a very sunken face, all very unnerving, and then a dog ran past me, this also came from my left hand side.

There were also dark moving shadows on the door, this whole experience lasted a good five minutes and it only ceased when we had stopped talking about the suicide.

And afterwards I felt very confused.

Maureen and I were a little shaken by the above events to say the least.

Joe Archer by Roy Walters

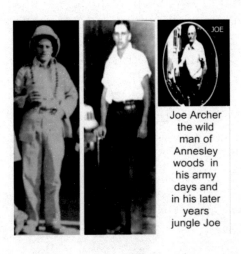

Joe Archer
the wild
man of
Annesley
woods in
his army
days and
in his later
years
jungle Joe

Does the wild man of Annesly woods, Joe archer known far and wide as jungle Joe, still roam Annesly woods? Patrolling and still doing his rounds as head woodsman, [self appointed I may add but that matters not.] Over a quarter of a century down the road since Joe made his last patrol, of Annesly woods Or was It.? I think not. Joe made his home in wood land at the side of Gipsy lane, and more or less lived the life of a recluse. The stories of Joe Archer have travelled far and wide, up and down the country, North, South, East, and West. Someone, somewhere, speaks Joe's name, as Joes old war stories keep resurfacing, the life he lived as a child, and the long winding road of his life. I have heard his name, and his adventures spring from many lips. But what do people really know about old Joe; well I will tell you I will fill a few little gaps in. The great Joe Saab as we used to call him when I was a kid is my uncle. I can tell you this as well; there is a lot more to Annesly woods than meets the eye, as Joe knows all too well. I think when Joe stepped in to this world a lot of people rubbed their heads, and rightly so. My Mother Ivy Walters, nee Archer, Joes Sister, as told me many a story about JOE. He would on many occasions call in to our house, on his way up to Annesly woods , when he had been down Hucknall,town shopping or shifting a swift pint or two, or three, he liked a pint now and then did Joe. My Mam would put him some dinner out and we would get him telling us all about his adventures overseas, no doubt some of them stretched a mile or two but the foundations of the stories were there. A little about Joe and his family, Joe was named after his dad [my granddad Joe]. They lived at 2a Victoria Street Hucknall Notts. Joe's mothers name was Elizabeth, granddads second wife, a quiet but stern lady. Joe's brothers where, Norbert better known by his nick name as Rab, a plasterer by trade. Served many years in the army, proudly serving his country was also a P.O.W. was a very keen gardener, and had a passion for motor bikes, having himself a 650 B.S.A. Ivan known to many as trot, also a very keen gardener, a quiet man and described by many as the salt of the earth. Also Sid and Jack. Joe also had three sisters Rita, who sadly passed at just five years old. Maud, and my Mother Ivy, better known as fan. Joe's dad lived to a ripe old age of 88, leaving us in AUGUST 1961. Joe comes from a big family, has is dad was married twice, so Joe also has half brothers and sisters in addition to his immediate family . Joe also has family in Australia, New –Zealand, and Ireland. In 1881, Joe senior, was living in Mansfield, at 11 new gate streets. Getting back to Joe, he has always lived on the wilder side of life, and was more at home with Mother Nature than he was with People. Joe loved the solitude of the woods, and made Annesly woods, his home for the last 30 odd years of his life. But Joe lived outside for most of his life, even as a child. No doubt about it Joe was the wild card. True he had many a fall outs with his family, but then again who don't? He was his own man, had his own mind, and from time to time, Joe would speak his mind discharging both barrels if need be. But under all the rough and tumble, he was well liked by a lot of people, he lived his life to the full no time wasted with this man, every breath he drew he lived it. Joe served his country well, with over 15 years of army service under his belt. Serving in Burma, India, Crete, Palestine, Syria and Egypt. You name it and Joes been there, and if he has not been, then it's not worth going any way. Trained rigorously in jungle fighting, he was a raw boned strong young,man and even in his twilight years was the old bull of the wilds. Even Joes old rocking boots, have been the topic of many a conversations. They were repaired that much, new souls being stuck on the bottom of the boots in the middle over the top of all the,others made his boots like rocking boots. When he threw his boots off on to the floor, they would rock back and forth, like an old rocking chair you know to say Joe lived with nature would be an understatement, Joe was nature. The cats and dogs that lived with Joe in the woods, where all wild. Strays that he took in, and shared his food with. Yes he would eat hedgehog, squirrel, and many other wild animals, but he lived a lot off the Land, and would only kill, to eat. He washed and bathed in the stream in all weathers, rain wind, sleet, or snow Joe was all part of it. No homely comforts for Joe. No Electricity, gas, television, or radio, he got his light from hurricane lamps and candles, cooked his food outside on open fires, life was hard But Joe was harder. Joe did live on and off over the years with his family, but he was a hard man to live with by any standards. One time he set the house on fire by making a fire in the middle of the bedroom floor, and many a time he would put something on the stove to cook, then decide to go a walk over Misk-hills or up and over the meadow, which he called Joe Saabs happy hunting grounds ,or where ever his mind would take him, returning hours later to holes burnt right through sauce pans, yes he done some crazy things a lot of them I can't write about it would be carving the joint a bit too close to the bone so to speak , but Joe was Joe, he was one on his own . Joes dad was still working at Linby pit, when he was 71, then got a job at Raleigh, the bike factory till he was 77, another tough old boot, I think Joe junior was a chip off the old block . Joe lived in the woods just off gipsy lane, and done much work on the surrounding farms, he was also an x miner, and worked for ford and western, labouring for a few years. One evening granddad came upon a queue of people stretching right down his entry, and on to the street, Victoria street ,that is, he asked what was going off ,why were they all there they said we have come to watch Joes boxing match ,what boxing match granddad asks, they pointed up to Joes bedroom window , where he had displayed a large sign Advertising a boxing match ,taking on all comers at 7 o clock, entry fee five shillings, granddad had to move them all off, this was just one of Joes many carry ones, I suppose granddad just took it all in his stride, he was that sort of man . Even when Joe lived at home with his family, most of the time he would cook on the back garden putting bricks round and preferring to cook his food outside, and he would do this in all weathers. Down the bottom of the garden in an old shed ,he would have chickens, and other things and an old Billy goat, he had in tow, I think he bought it to get his own milk, but never got any with it being a Billy goat and not a nanny goat but that's best left alone . Then there was the time Joe was riding his bike, Joes old bone shaker, as he used to call it. Well Joes old bone shaker was rattling along down the motor way till the police pulled him up no lights, no brakes, he used to jump off it and run with it till he could stop it, the fine he got clearly spelt out to Joe, you can't go on the motor way on a push bike . I wonder how many people have had some of Joes famous stews, he used to boil up on his outdoor fires in the woods, I think anything that moved or did not move went in to his stew, even dog meat old bits of burnt wood, all added to the flavour any creepy crawlies that fell in stayed there, but it never did Joe any harm it kept him warm in Winter. I asked Joe years ago, what it was like living in the woods especially at night , he told me there where evil things in these woods which he said he had Encountered on numerous occasions, things he said that would frighten any man to death by just seeing them . When I asked what? He said if I told you what was in these woods, you would never step foot in them again not even in day time, never mind the night. I said what then ghosts, he said what I've seen in these woods at night, would frighten even ghosts. He said he as stood face to face with pure evil in the woods at night, but would not say what. Was this one of Joe's tall stories I don't know? But other people I know have also said there are horrible things in Annesly-woods, so as Joe seen and confronted what other people have only heard about. Joe did touch on the dark arts that he said have been practiced in the woods with sinister Intent. Saying he as stumbled on Satanists at night in the woods gathering and invoking, malevolent powers which brings to mind when I was over in Bestwood woods, over near the little church in the woods the care taker there, was telling me about groups of Satanists, gathering over there at night, and had been desecrating the graves .Annesly- woods is only a Stone's throw away, so there could be a lot of truth in what Joe says .he told me a bit about black magic rituals, and about witch doctors, and Voo doo which he seemed to know a great deal about from his army days, and the different countries he had been to . When I pressed him again on Annesly-woods he said, I leave them alone, they leave me alone and I suppose those who do dabble in such things will pay the piper . I have spoken to three people in Hucknall who do know about these things, and Annesly woods only to be told Roy, keep out them woods, especially at night. Well they do know a lot more than what I do and they would not enlighten me any further. BUT IT DOES GIVE YOU FOOD FOR THOUGHT. Joe's body had to be identified by those old boots he wore, and the coroner recorded an open verdict. If only those old famous rocking boots of Joes could talk, they might shed a little more light on Annesly-woods. A few short years ago I saw a map in HUCKNALL Library referring to the woods just off gypsy lane where Joe used to live, which was now referred to as DEAD MANS WOOD.

Not a Good Feeling by Roy Walters

On Monday evening 26th of July 2010 time roughly 9-15 pm Alan smith and I set out to go over the old misk hills to undertake a paranormal investigation in certain areas however when we arrived over in the vicinity we discovered our way barred

So with that we decided to change our plans slightly and revisit another destination

That being once again Linby village and Papplewick

Where in the past we have gathered a mountain of paranormal phenomena ranging from photographs of strange mists, orbs, very intense balls of light in the hedgerow and sky, also disembodied voices, and a whole array of phenomena

Our visit that evening proved yet again to be a very strange evening, we both Alan and myself being a little taken back to say the least by events that slowly unfolded that evening

events as such as we walked on to the public foot path leading through to Papplewick church

Alan started to feel something around him mostly around his back with pressure on the back of his neck, Alan being a spirit medium is very susceptible to spirit presence

Then he saw a black mist drift over the field something he has not seen before

he then became aware of a man dressed all in black some twenty feet away on the path

at this point I could see nothing or feel anything Alan stated that it was being impressed in his mind that the man was going to the church he also had the impression that the man was from the 18th century

I continued to take photographs just picking up orbs as I was talking to Alan I saw a man in dark clothing about fifteen feet in front of me just step in to the hedgerow which was a bit of a shock as there was only Alan and myself there and you could see right up the path way in front of you I stopped talking and was just looking to where I saw the man go

Alan then said to me have you just seen what I've just seen so I asked him what he just saw he said a man in dark clothing just walk in to the hedgerow so we had both just seen the same thing at the same time, there was no break in the hedgerow at this point and the hedge is very dense

I walked to where I had saw the man ,taking photographs but there was nothing on them and as I was walking to where I saw the man I said come on show yourself again

Then a cold line and that is the only way I can describe it, came straight through the crown of my head right from above me and went right down my spine to my feet ,it felt very disturbing I turned around and walked away from it back towards where Alan was standing ,as I did so this cold line that had come in to my body through my head left me but then I started to get pains for no apparent reason to the side of my left temple, not server but uncomfortable all the same

Alan was feeling discomfort to the back of his neck

He then asked out if we should go further down the field to which he got a distinct no

I saw a hand in my mind's eye rocking from side to side and I got the word iffy which ment to me it would be unwise to continue but no reason was given, I asked out again and got the word barrier in my mind and not to continue any further was being impressed on Alan

So with that we left the area, but before doing so we did say a prayer and asked for the area to be cleared of all negative energies

We have both experienced a lot of strange unexplainable phenomena in the said areas, over a considerable length of time.

One evening we both heard at the same time a woman humming a tune just at the side of us, but saw no one, but there was no uneasy feeling in the air like there was on the 26th of July, it may have been the anniversary of some unpleasantness that may have happened years ago we don't know and maybe never will.

One thing for certain, something was very much amiss that evening

Photos of Mist by Roy Walters

This photograph was taken on a clear June evening by Alan Smith.

No mist was visible to the eye, but as you can see from the photograph,

The mist is very intense all around me.

This photograph was taken on the back garden of my partner's house by me again the mist was not visible to the eye

I took this photograph, as we were coming off the field, hoping to get some orbs Around Alan, but I got all this mist around him and yet again, it could not be seen with the eye.

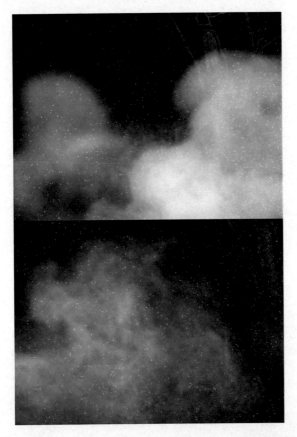

These two photographs, were taken by me, and again they were not visible to the eye .I took another photograph, only seconds later but there was nothing there, once again you Can see how thick this mist is, but it seems it's only visible to the camera.

Stepping Into Death by Tracey Griffiths

MELCHZADEK
DIVINE INTERVENTION

SUNDAY AUGUEST 26th 2003
WAS THE DAY MY EIGHT
YEAR OLD SON DIED AND
MY WHOLE LIFE JUST
CALLASPED AND DIED
THERE WITH HIM
THEN JESUS STEPPED
FORWARD AND BREATHED
LIFE BACK IN TO MY SON.
YES MIRACLES DO STILL
HAPPEN.

Although nothing could have prepared me for the horrible events that took place on Sunday August 26th 2003, there were certainly many indicators that something major was about to go down. It wasn't until after the event though that the significance of these things became obvious. The first strange happening took place at my Mother's house in Feb 2003.My then 8 year old son started shouting from the garden, 'Mum!' 'Mum comes quickly!'I didn't take too much notice. But he persisted. 'Mum! Quick! Look at this!!'He then ran inside. 'Quick Mum! Come! Jesus is in the garden!''Yeah, right' I laughed. He kept on going, so eventually. Mainly to get some peace I went out to see what had got him so excited. As I expected there was nothing there. He was so insistent though that he'd seen Jesus & was pointing to the exact spot and rattling off a description that I knew he'd seen something. Mums house backs onto bush and a creek that further upstream adjoins a Mental Institution, & when fronted with a description of an old man with long robes and a sceptre lurking in the yard my first thought was 'wandering Mental patient' & it wouldn't have been the first time we'd had to lock ourselves in and have someone collected. I ushered him inside and didn't give it another thought. In the months leading up to Jimmies accident he had started complaining of shooting pains like pins and needles throughout his body, was breaking out in random small bruises and having palpitations so severe that you could see his heart thumping in his chest. Doctors tested him for everything from simple Iron levels to Leukaemia and Neurological disorders and couldn't find anything wrong. Ironically, he has not had a recurrence of these symptoms since. I feel that in some subconscious way his body was aware of what was to come and was preparing him for the impact. In the year leading up to my son's accident I had become almost obsessed with studying the planetary aspects of those that had suffered sudden and violent deaths. To my horror I saw that my sons Natal Astrology chart contained a Grand Cross, which is a grim, burden like aspect suggesting he would have some 'cross to bear' in his life/While I was frantically studying his chart trying to ascertain 'what' would happen and 'when', It happened. Since I was 13 years old I have been reading Tarot cards and for 2 months prior to Jimmies accident the cards were clearly showing hospitalization of a child. Although I knew something was coming, I still had no idea at all that it would be MY child, or that it would be so serious. The next blinding indicator that something big was about to happen was THE DREAM. One of those dreams you wake up from and KNOW you've had a really important and meaningful dream. It went like this; I found myself sitting in the local Cemetery in a large multilevel oval row of seating like you'd see in a sports arena. It looked out onto a field of graves. It was a sunny day & I felt happy & at peace. For some reason I was there to get a present for my Mothers birthday. I walked to a nearby stall where every item was emblazoned with a symbol of a stick figure playing sport; it's the local Councils sports and recreation logo. I sat back in the seats overlooking the graves with the goblet I'd just bought and looked to my left. There was a high wall and my Son was racing round on top of it. I shouted to him to get down before he fell, just then, a huge, dark freak wave flew up and pulled him into the water. I ran to the wall screaming and an Indian man beside me jumped in and started looking for him. The man surfaced a couple of times to tell me it was no good, he couldn't find him. He then started climbing out of the water. I was panicked, & grabbed him by the shirt. 'Well ****in try again!!!!' I screamed at him as I hurled him back into the water. I woke up shaking, and made a mental note to watch Jami like a hawk around water. Although the Universe was throwing massive Omens out there to me, each one getting more and more to the point that something awful was about to happen, I still remained blissfully oblivious. So the Universe sent me 1 last blindingly obvious Omen, which again, I dismissed as ridiculous. While walking down the street, about 2 weeks prior to the accident, a vision of my son, entangled up high in power lines flashed into my head."UGu! Where did that come from?" I thought, and blocked that thought just as quickly as it came. The Universe gave up about then in disgust I think. Sunday 26th August came, and right up until I heard the bang, it was a blissful day. The Sun was shining, the housework was done, and the bills were paid. The kids were playing happily outside, the stereo was cranking and all was well in my world. My Son and a group of friends came in and asked if they could play at a house across the road. We walked down to the road, I watched them go safely across the road and knock on the door. Just then an old friend pulled into the drive that I hadn't seen for ages. I welcomed him in and put the jug on. Two sips into my cup of coffee we hear a bang so loud it sounded like thunder, and the whole area seemed to shake. Part of me didn't want to go outside and look, but I knew I had to go outside. The sound was so ungodly that I was fully expecting to go out and see a car accident or similar, but I certainly never expected to see my then 8 year old Son 7 metres up in the air being electrocuted by an 11000 volt High Voltage Power line! From thereon, everything seemed to go in still frame slow motion, even though, from the time of me screaming and running outside, to us leaving in a convoy of ambulances and Paramedics with sirens screaming took all of 6 minutes. As I watched the Power line release him, and watched him slump lifelessly to the ground I remember screaming for an ambulance and trying to keep calm. I could see by his injuries he was past saving, but I kept going with trying to stay calm as I knew Hysteria on my part would just screw everything and slow down the whole process of getting him to Hospital. The details of the accident scene are far too graphic and gory to include in this story, so I will leave a lot out unless it's relevant to the story. I cleared his airway and loosened his clothing, knowing my next step was to check for a pulse and start CPR .At this point I froze. It was plain from his still chest, and the fact that it was aflame and had a hole blown through it, and many more injuries that were equally serious that I wasn't going to find a pulse. This would confirm his death, I couldn't bear to find no pulse, the hysteria was coming at the thought of it, and Panic was setting in. Luckily for me, and Jami, My Indian neighbour appeared from nowhere, jumped in and started resuscitation. At first it wasn't working, I couldn't bear to watch and ran inside to call an ambulance just in case no one had. I came back just in time to see him splutter back into consciousness, convulse briefly and lose consciousness again. Ambulances soon surrounded the scene, our next mission was to keep him alive for the next 30 minutes, which we all seriously doubted we could do, but we did it. We were met at the hospital by a team of surgeons who immediately whisked him away and started work. Lots of family and friends came up to the hospital, I remember someone suggesting we prayed... I thought this was a good idea, a short time later I looked up to find that four whole hours had passed and I hadn't even noticed. The news wasn't good, but he was at least still alive. We had to amputate his arm to the shoulder do emergency skin grafts and take a small part of his Liver and put him in a drug induced coma on life support if he was even to last the night. There was no option but to sign the consent forms and keep up the silent praying. Luckily for us, there was a LOT of praying going on, WORLDWIDE, we had Christians, Buddhists, Mormons, pagans, Jehovah's witnesses, Baptists, spiritualists, you name them, they were praying. The local Buddhist Centre even did special blessing ceremonies for him. Between the ongoing daily surgeries and constant spiritual healing and prayer, SOMETHING pulled him through and within a couple of weeks he was although critically injured out of his coma and able to talk. He recalled what he saw at the accident scene. He tried to call out to me, next he saw and heard a whole lot of black and white stuff that hissed and went right through him (from what he described Id liken it to the white noise and fuzzy grey screen you see in an unturned TV, like white noise),Then he felt weird like he was falling. When he got up, he describes seeing a really bright yellowy white light with hundreds of people standing amongst it... He then spoke of walking around me and talking to me, but getting annoyed as I was ignoring him and just looking at the ground and crying. I asked him if he could see what I was looking at, he replied that he couldn't, all he could see was a shadow on the ground in front of me. I asked if he knew any of the people standing in the light. He didn't know them, but when he described them to me I recognized my Dad, my Grandma, my Granddad and a friend who'd passed from cancer in previous years but whom he still would have been too young to remember. That man was there too,' he said. 'The one from Grandmas garden'. Next he describes feeling 'weird' and waking up to find our neighbour 'kissing him' then he looks accusingly at me and says' and you were letting him'. I knew now that the man in Grandmas Garden was no mental patient, perhaps he HAD seen Jesus. Was the Indian man in my dream the same man who saved him? The Council Logo in the dream mirrored the fact that it was a Council owned tree he climbed when he was injured. Everything was starting to fit. I asked him if the man said anything to him. He said 'yeah, well sort of. His mouth wasn't moving, but I could hear his voice, like he was talking in my head. 'What did he say? I asked. 'Well, it was weird, it wasn't even a word really, it was stupid, he just said Aloha, or Aloha's been quite excited, no 8 year old or indeed most people without religious background would know a word like that. Indeed at that point I also didn't fully know what it meant; I'd seen it written on church signs and in the bible. We were determined to find out who the mystery man was. and what Aloha meant. Over the next few days, every opportunity I got I downloaded every possible Saint, Avatar, Ascended master and religious Icon picture I could get my hands on and took the laptop to the hospital. After sorting through dozens of Ascended masters and biblical characters he spotted his man! That's him! He said excitedly. The man's name was Melchizadek, or Melchizadec depending on which website you visited. According to the text he was an ancient being from the old testament days referred to as the beginning and the end, the alpha and the Omega, in a nutshell one of the earliest incarnations as what we know as Jesus. And Aloha was the collective seven rays of the healing light of God; an Aloha was a single ray of the healing light of God. After that day, Jami has only sighted Melchizadek on one more occasion, it was a surgery we both feared he wouldn't make it through, but thanks to Melchizadek he did. The accident seemed to have an enhancing effect on his esp., for about 18 months or so he would regularly describe people I couldn't see wandering through the house, but who I could recognize by description. Obviously God has something quite special lined up for Jami to send someone as important as Melchizadek to ensure his safety, has 14 now, so no doubt the next few decades will reveal what his special purpose is.

Layton Burrow by Roy Walters

Photo of Rosemary School Mansfield

Life hands out' many experiences for all of us. Some good, some bad, some happy, and some sad, some very funny, and some very frightening, throughout life, most of us have our fair share. But when I reflect back to my childhood, a lot of my experiences were worrying, and very frightening, because most of my child hood revolved around ghosts, spirits, strange happenings, and poverty. All the ghostly things, I had no understanding of, with just being a kid and in those days who could you talk to, about such things. It's hard enough today nearly half a century on. You still come up against (THAT LOOK) from a lot of people. Even in this day and age, people's minds are so tightly closed. I suppose what happens to you as a child, does shape you as an adult. As I fall back through my mind yet once again, the years start to fall away. Far back along the dusty road of time, the early 1960s stares right back at me. I was at the fresh hold of the biggest change in my life. I resided NO more at PadleyHall, on a permanent basis. It was still home to my family but not me. My new home became Layton Burrow, Mansfield. A beautiful seven bed roomed property, that stood in its own grounds had its own lawned tennis court, large gardens; to me it was a palace. In reality it was a children's home. But to me it was a complete new world, a new way of life. No ghosts to scare me half to death, or so I thought. I attended Rosemary school, on Rosemary Street, an old Victorian school, but I loved it, every single day I was there, the best three years of my life without a shadow of a doubt. But in the cellar at Layton Burrow, something lurked. The cellar consisted of three large rooms, four actually ,as there was a brick out in one of the a joining walls, on shining a torch through the hole it revealed yet another large room, so the cellar must have gone under the whole house . The house was a beautiful home, I thought quiet serene. But the cellar was something else. I had to go down in this cellar many times, over the three years I lived at Layton burrow. Each week we all had different jobs to do, i.e. one week you would be on washing up, another week on setting the tables, every meal time another week peeling spuds, then a week on coal and coke, which consisted of getting coal and coke up all week from the cellar, to keep the fires and boiler going . Most people did not like this job, I think they were all afraid of the cellar but me, I hated it, I could always feel something in there, and even more so on the cellar steps, than in the cellar. One day I was down there getting coke for the boiler, I could feel some one very close to me, at the back of me, I went very cold, I was too scared to turn round, I had a tremendous strong feeling of being watched intently, I quickly scooped the coke up in to the scuttles , then something touched my back, there was nothing behind me, only empty space , and most probably a cloud of dust as I shot up the cellar steps, but half way up them , I went through something freezing cold, I had passed right through something, that could not be seen, but certainly could be felt, I shuddered all through my body, once through the door at the top of the cellar steps, it was like stepping in to a whole new world . I used to think that something had followed me from padley hall, like it had come looking for me, and was hiding in the cellar, but I now know that was not the case, it's just that I am a bit sensitive to spirit but as a child, I had no understanding of this. Many a time while at school, I would see dark shapes of people out the corner of my eye, turn towards them, and they would be gone, looking back it was most probably people, who have been and gone, and revisiting there old school, I know I certainly would . I remember one day, I was in the play ground with a friend, when I saw a dark shape, a little bit bigger than he was, it was sort of fluttering at the back of him, then moving to his right, then his left, you could not see it as a person, it was more like a dark hazy thing, after a few moments it had gone, but a few days later his grandmother died, I don't know if there was any connection with this . One day I met some friends from school, and we went in to this old empty house, there was about five of us, any way we went up the stairs in this old house, just messing about as kids do. There were all rubbish piled up at the bedroom door, old furniture and an old mattress, you had to climb over it all, to get in to the bed room, Some of my friends were scrambling over the top, I was just about to, when I felt some one right at the back of me very angry, I think it was a woman saying without words, get out, get out, I had never felt anything so strong as this, it was like she was screaming at you . My friends just carried on oblivious to anything, the word get out was very angrily forced in to my head, I presume by someone who lived and died there and was very attached to the place, we would be seen as intruders, but to us kids it was just an old empty house . But still very much a home, to the spirits that still resided there. I said I am going out, and I quickly went down the stairs and out the door, my mates quickly followed me, but I said nothing to them , we walked over this waste land, I turned and looked back at the house and we were quiet away from it then, but as soon as I looked at the house, I felt something staring right back at me with such anger and it was not imagination running wild, I really felt it ,it, was like eyes boring in to you. That was over 44 years ago now, and it's as clear today as it ever was. There were six or seven of us out one night myself and john seven, friends from school, Kenny flowers, Dave Thurman, Joan drake, and a very close special friend of mine, Barbara Brocklehurst . I wanted desperately to tell her about all these things that had happened to me at padley hall, and all the other things I felt and saw on many occasions, I know she was the only one who would not laugh at me , and think I was some kind of nut case, but I did not know how to start and tell her, and I was very shy at that time, I waited for a time when we were more or less on our own, and I thought after three so I counted 123 in my head, then just said Brock do you believe in ghost, then just waited but she did not respond to me, she just looked at me , we all ways just looked in to each other's eyes but said nothing but that is another story, any way I thought she did not hear me, then I felt really daft and could not find the courage to ask her again . If only she had answered me, I would have had someone to talk to about all the things that scared me, and had done for years, I could have told her all about padley hall, and the things I used to see at school and in the cellar, and all about the night mares, I used to have, but it was just not to be. May be she would not of understood at her age, as we were both only thirteen then, but at least I would have had someone to talk to about it I'm fifty eight now, not much has changed, I've just got older and spirit still come around me sometimes, I get a little concerned but take most things in my stride, I have not been physically hurt to date by them but having said that my partner Barbara has.

Visitors From The Other Side
Contributed by John Roberts.

We moved into the house in Feb 93 and it was approx. 25 yrs old at that time. Soon after moving in we would sometimes notice bright flashes of light in the living room which had no explanation and our dog would sit growling at one corner of the ceiling. We had only a tiny back garden (a postage stamp really) so we had put stones down over the old lawn and they covered 90 % with a small patio by the back door. On quite regular evenings we would hear footsteps crunching over the stones and then they would step onto the patio (thankfully no further) this was witnessed by relatives and neighbours too.

My wife was cleaning bedrooms upstairs one day and both the kids were playing out front in her view; she heard a small child giggling at the bottom of the stairs and the noise then moved up the stairs and into the main bedroom. My wife was in the rear bedroom and was so frightened she froze at first but then ran round checking the house and no one was there. Our phone was situated in the hallway between the kitchen and living room. I was on the phone when a small, blonde girl of about 6 ran past me into the living room, actually bumping my leg; at first I just assumed it was my daughter who was around that age, but then I realized that this girl was smaller so I looked into the l. room from which there was only one other exit via a very heavy and complicated "tilt and slide" door- no one was there. She couldn't have opened the T and S door and she never came back past me so where did she go? She was seen by my father on one occasion when he was staying with us (in the living room). He woke early to find her standing at the bottom of the sofa bed- he was pretty scared. The child just looked normal and was in clothes that looked contempary. We always knew she was around because we could smell something like sweet sherbet- you could literally pin the smell down to a foot square area and it would move around.

My brother had probably the only really frightening incident with her. He came to stay with us intending this to be for quite a long while (he had cheated on his wife and been caught!). We had a large kitchen diner and my wife had split it in two with a shelving unit and up t him a bed behind it. At the bottom of the bed was the table. He woke one night to find the blankets being pulled from the bottom of the bed which he first thought was our greyhound rolling over (she always slept under the table), but he realised Sandy was over by the sink shivering with fear. The next night he heard a woman's voice out in the hall and thought my wife was on the telephone but then the voice was suddenly in the room with him and the bed clothes were being pulled off again. The voice said (we presume to the little girl)" doesn't do that you'll scare him". At this time he had not told us about this but the following night he was in the hallway on the telephone very late at night trying to talk his wife round, a photo flew up and smashed into his face- we presume the ghost(s) didn't approve of his conduct. He left our house the next day and never returned!

Not long before we moved from there we visited London. No one was in or had access to our house but when we returned my daughter shouted down "who moved my bed?" Her bed had been shoved against the window and all her teddies had been stacked behind it.

On another occasion we had again been to London and her curtains wouldn't close- something must have removed the curtain rail from the wall and tucked all the tab top curtains behind the screws

The final event, one week before we left was; my son had stayed the night at his friend's and when we woke we noticed that his door was closed. At first we thought our daughter was in there but she was in her own bed. We inched the door open and saw that in an empty room something had pushed the wardrobe between the bottom of the bed and the door leaving us only fingertip room to push the wardrobe away.

The little girl also visited our neighbour 2 doors away- we have sat in her kitchen in an empty house listening to all the doors and drawers slamming in and out in the bedroom. She eventually called in the spiritualist church who blessed it.

We tried to research the history of the house. There were no deaths on record and the land was previously farm land but whilst laying the stones in the garden a neighbour told us there used to be a playground on the site and we dug up the base to a seesaw. Despite going through archives at the library right back to 1900 we never found out who she was

These events took place at our home in Whernside in Rugby over an eleven year period by John Roberts.

About The Author

Born at Victoria hospital, in Mansfield, on the 12th of August 1951.

Born in to a large family, being one of ten children.

Lived in HUCKNALL most of his life.

At the age of 12 years old, returned to Mansfield, where he attended Rosemary school, on Rosemary Street, living at 17 Layton burrow, children's home, returning back to HUCKNALL, on leavening school, worked as a metal polisher, for many years, also an x miner.

Written and published, many articles, on various subjects, over the years.

Once described by a very prominent gentleman, as being and I quote,

A proper English gentleman, with a heart of gold, but a bit rough around the edges.

Been involved with spiritualism, and the paranormal, for many years.

Now retired due to ill health, enjoys participating, in paranormal investigations.

Spent most of his life, helping others, proud father of eight children.